# Jeff Galloway

## Running—Testing Yourself

# Jeff Galloway

*Running—*

*Testing Yourself*

MEYER
& MEYER
SPORT

British Library Cataloguing in Publication Data
A catalogue record for this book is available from the British Library

Jeff Galloway—Testing Yourself
Oxford: Meyer & Meyer Sport (UK) Ltd., 2005
ISBN 1-84126-167-X

© 2005 by Meyer & Meyer Sport (UK) Ltd.
Aachen, Adelaide, Auckland, Budapest, Graz, Johannesburg,
New York, Olten (CH), Oxford, Singapore, Toronto
Member of the World
Sports Publishers' Association (WSPA)
www.w-s-p-a.org
Printed and bound by: TZ Verlag, Germany
ISBN 1-84126-167-X
E-Mail: verlag@m-m-sports.com
www.m-m-sports.com

# CONTENTS

# INTRODUCTION

I've had the good fortune to live a lifestyle that is full of running. At first I enjoyed overcoming the challenges of competition and time improvement. Today, I appreciate even more the daily boost of vitality and mental focus that I've not found in any other activity for about 50 years. In 1958, however, it was very improbable that I would run at all. I was an under-active, overweight 13 year old taking my first continuous running steps, full of exertion anxiety. I struggled to complete every one of the first month's workouts. Why did I continue? At first, it was the unexpected deep-seeded, feeling of self worth that was delivered after every run.

As I learned to push myself to the limits of my capabilities, during high school and college years, there were always a few runs every week that were enjoyable. But on the really tough days, I was often frustrated by seeing others run faster who didn't work as hard. Because I was an average runner who wanted to get a little better, I read and questioned other runners, and tried many different types of workouts. What kept me going were the supportive friendships I found in each running group. Between the shared jokes, free doses of philosophy, and daily solving of the world's problems, practically every run left me feeling like I had bonded with the other runners in a special way. I feel the same way today, even when I am coaching other runners via email. There is a positive chemistry when runners get together, tending to bring out the best in each, usually leading to the desire to help one another.

During my most competitive years, I learned that the improvement process was due mostly to not giving up. As I read, questioned other runners, experimented and adjusted, I quickly discovered that there were many paths to the same goal. Yes, I was continually going through ups and downs—including hundreds of injuries. The "downs" weren't fun, but were the most important component of my running development: I learned much more from the mistakes than from the successes.

At first, I didn't enjoy testing myself. But once I learned how important it was for a competitor to know current fitness potential, I first came to appreciate, and then enjoy the test experience. The challenge of each week's key workout stimulated me to get better, and the races and tests were the reality checks that helped me fine-tune my training.

I now believe that because I tested myself regularly, I was better able to put together the thousands of running experiences into an understandable improvement plan. This resulted in my making the '72 Olympic team. If there was one piece of the mosaic that was more important, it was the ability to pace correctly under various weather conditions. The weekly tests taught me how to set realistic goals, and then to run my own race through proper pacing.

The information in this book is offered as advice from one runner to another—and not as medical fact. The principles were learned during the 14 years I spent becoming an Olympian. They have been enhanced, reinforced and expanded many times over from my work with over 150,000 average people, who have tested themselves through using my methods.

Above all, I salute all who put themselves to a realistic challenge. If you haven't done this, you have one of life's great rewards waiting for you. By choosing realistic goals, training within your limits, and then putting yourself to a meaningful challenge, you'll find find that you have much more strength inside than you thought.

# WHY DO WE TEST OURSELVES?

When you balance stress and rest, running bestows a sense of satisfaction and achievement that is unsurpassed. Intuitively, we know that this is good for us, mentally and physically. When we decide to take on the challenge of getting better, we tap into a mysterious and complex part of us: the human spirit. Once embarked on this journey, we look on running and life in a different way. Simply stated, we expect more out of each.

The mission of improvement starts for many when the fitness honeymoon ends. Over several months or years, a runner notices and enjoys a variety of physical and mental benefits. But at some point, virtually every runner will hit a wall of boredom or low motivation. Sometimes this comes in the form of envy of others who started when you did, but are running faster finish times. Beware of trying to emulate a faster runner: Usually speed is due to having made a better choice of parents. But the reality is that when runners look for something to add spice to their running, they often choose a time goal.

**Why can't I run faster?**  Those who act on this thought, often don't have a clue about their limits, and usually exceed them. This leads to physical problems and a loss of motivation initially. Then come the inevitable questions as to why the aches, pains, injury, or burnout. With a little more awareness of your capabilities, you're ready for a revised and more realistic vision. This is accomplished by testing yourself.

Having worked with so many people who have made this journey, I want to assure you that it doesn't have to take a lot of time, or produce debilitating fatigue. The methods in this book have been used successfully by thousands of runners with wide ranges of ability and not much time to train. If you use the tests and the training program to prepare for and predict performance realistically, you will have an invaluable way to manage your improvement.

I've noticed that there is a competitor hidden inside even the most sedentary person. Something inside us wants us to be more fit, and once we've established a base, that something wants us to push a little. After several more months of tests, the same internal programming gets us thinking about becoming the best we can be.

**Warning: you may experience addiction.** The process of gently and regularly challenging yourself stimulates a desire to question priorities, use time and energy more efficiently, and extend your capabilities. This can work its way into other areas of life. Once feeling the benefits, you don't want to go back to lazier days. It's a good addiction, but many runners say that they consistently feel the pull to make themselves better in some way—and they blame their running for initiating this.

**Learn your limits.** Most people go through their lives without a clue whether they could push themselves to physical limits, and no concept about how to do this safely. The series of gentle running tests in this book, will gradually push you into a series of unknowns. Since each person can control the effort level, your body tells you when you're pushing too hard. The testing process involves guessing and adjusting, going too far and then backing off. When done each week, the body organism makes adaptations so that you get better at judging pace at the beginning, and knowing when you can push further or should drop back (to avoid much greater drops later). The overall experience of doing this, even for one season, progressively reduces anxiety of the unknown as it develops confidence in confronting limitations in other areas.

**Beware of the ego.** Some of the most timid beginning runners have become some of the most aggressive competitors I've worked with. As you find your times improving through regular training, the ego starts telling you things you want to hear. "If you improved 10 seconds with one weekly speed workout, then two hard workouts will double the improvement." Many runners have let the ego take away their enjoyment of a gentle run—pushing them farther and faster on days that should have been reserved for slow recovery. Once they started racing, the ego told them that lap times in workouts or in races could bestow greater satisfaction. Beware of this line of thinking. The inevitable slower races will trigger disappointment, while faster times most often lead to a yearning for even faster times.

It is healthy to let your ego have its moments of glory as you perform well. Just realize that improvement is not continually an upward curve, and the ego has a problem with any downturn. A natural selection process occurs during a speed training season, as the ego is forced to deal with reality, and make adjustments. But by maintaining the enjoyment of a fun run every week, and appreciating the afterglow from any run, you can maintain a balanced set of rewards, while keeping the ego in check.

While testing yourself for faster times can keep you focused, and may increase motivation, the blending of mind body and spirit is maintained primarily through the enjoyment of the act of running—usually on slow runs, and in the slow warm up and warm down jogs that bracket your workouts. Year-to-year, I've experienced an almost continuous stream of enjoyment from running for about half a century. It keeps getting better because I have regular doses of enjoyable runs. Even when I was training for the Olympics, about 90% of my weekly miles were spent running at a slow and enjoyable pace.

Performance increase is not a continuous upward trek. Be prepared to record times on at least half of your tests that are slower than you think you should be running. This is often due to the ego telling you to run faster than you are really able at that point in time. Be patient, learn from your setbacks, and you will generally move forward.

So take the leap of faith, and jump into the testing process. By pushing the limits you may learn more about yourself than in any other activity in life. The real treasure is ahead: finding hidden strengths that help you get through even the toughest of tests in life.

# IMPORTANT NOTES BEFORE YOU GET STARTED

## Medical check?

Check with your doctor's office before you start any strenuous training program. Just tell the doctor or head nurse that you plan to run regularly, with the idea of running some speed sessions every week. Almost every person will be given the green light. The doctor may or may not decide to give you a physical or exercise stress test. If your doctor recommends against running, ask why. Since there are so few people who should not do this, I suggest that you get a second opinion in this case. There may be a good reason, but the best medical advisor is one who wants you to do the physical activity that you want—unless there are medical reasons against it.

## Choosing a doctor

A growing number of family practice physicians are advocates for fitness. If your doctor is not very supportive, ask the nurses in the office and other sources (running stores, etc.) if there is another doctor who might be. The doctors who are physical fitness advocates are very often more postive and energetic about other areas of health promotion.

The running grapevine can help. Ask the staff at local running stores, running club members, or long-term runners. They will usually know of several doctors in your town who runners consult when they have a problem. Doctors tell me that, compared with their other patients, runners tend to ask more questions, and want to keep themselves in good health. You want a doctor who will welcome this, and serve as your "health coach," someone who will work with you to avoid injury, sickness, and other health setbacks. Doctors have also told me that runners tend to have fewer bouts with sickness.

## Heart disease and running

Running tends to have a protective effect from cardiovascular disease. But more runners die of heart disease than any other cause, and they are susceptible to the same risk factors as sedentary people. Like most other citizens, runners at risk usually don't know that they are. I know of a number of runners who have suffered heart attacks and strokes who probably could have prevented them if they had taken a few simple tests. Some of these are listed below, but check with your doctor if you have any questions or concerns.

Your heart is the most important organ in your body. This short section is offered as a guide to help you take charge over your heart to maintain a high level of health in the most important organ for longevity, and quality of life. As always, you need to get advice about your individual situation from a cardiologist who knows you and specializes in this area.

### Risk Factors—get checked if you have two of these—or one that is serious

- Family history
- Poor lifestyle habits earlier in life
- High fat/high cholesterol diet
- Have smoked—or still smoke
- Obese or severely overweight
- High blood pressure
- High cholesterol

### Tests

- Stress test—heart is monitored during a run that gradually increases in difficulty
- C reactive Protein—has been an indicator of increased risk
- Heart scan—an electronic scan of the heart which shows calcification, and possible narrowing of arteries
- Radioactive dye test—very effective in locating specific blockages; talk to your doctor about this
- Carotid ultrasound test—helps to prevent stroke
- Ankle-brachial test—plaque build-up in arteries throughout the body

None of these are fool proof. But by working with your cardiologist, you can increase your chance of living until the muscles just won't propel you further down the road—past the age of 100.

## Should I run when I have a cold?

There are so many individual health issues with a cold that you must talk with a doctor before you exercise when you have an infection.

*Lung infection—don't run!* A virus in the lungs can move into the heart and kill you. Lung infections are usually indicated by coughing.

*Common Cold?* There are many infections that initially indicate a normal cold but are not. At least call your doctor's office to get clearance before running. Be sure to explain how much you are running, and what, if any, medication you are taking.

*Infections of the throat and above the neck*—most runners will be given the OK, but check with the doctor.

## Risk of speed

There is an increased risk of both injuries and cardiovascular events during speed sessions. Be sure to get your doctor's OK before beginning a speed program. The advice inside is generally conservative, but when in doubt, take more rest, more days off, and run slower. In other words...be more conservative.

## Advice from one runner to another

This book was written from one runner to another and is the result of about 50 years of running, several decades of speed training, and having been the "coach" to more than 150,000 runners in one way or another. None of the advice inside is offered as medical advice. To get help in this area, see a doctor or appropriate medical expert.

# WHAT DO I NEED TO GET STARTED?

## Buy the training shoe first

**G**o to the running store in your area with the most experienced staff. You'll need a pair for long runs and easy running days. You may want to get a racing shoe (or light weight training shoe) later. Bring along your most worn pair of shoes (any shoes), and a pair of running shoes that has worked well for you. Wait until you are several weeks into your training before you decide to get a racing shoe if you feel you need one. See the shoe section in this book.

## Do I need a racing shoe?

In most cases, racing shoes only speed you up by a few seconds a mile—but this may be what you need to reach your goal. Run in your training shoes for a week or 3 before you try on some racing shoes. As you go through a separate fitting process for a racing shoe, be sure to read the shoe section of this book.

## A watch

There are a lot of good, inexpensive watches which will give you accurate times on your speed workouts and races. Any watch that has a stopwatch function will do the job. Be sure to ask the staff person in the store how to use the stopwatch. A few watches can make walk breaks easier by "beeping" after each running segment and then again after the walking segment. For more information on current watches that do this, go to www.RunInjuryFree.com.

## Clothing?

Yes, wear it! But except for temperature extremes, it's best to wear garments that are light and comfortable. There are several types of technical fibers that can improve the running experience. If you suffer from chaffing between the legs, lycra tights or "bike tights" can reduce or eliminate the problem. Those who sweat profusely should wear tops and underwear made of polypro, dryfit, coolmax, or similar material. This will move moisture away from the skin, allow for evaporation, and reduce the weight carried due to perspiration.

# THE INSIDE STORY ON GETTING FASTER

By running easily and regularly, the whole body works together to help you move more efficiently while you increase your positive health potential. Lungs become more efficient, the heart is strengthened. Oxygen is processed more efficiently into the blood, and the blood is pumped more effectively through the body. At the same time, your leg muscles, tendons, joints, etc., make up a strong and coordinated system to gradually do more work, and move you farther and faster down the road.

When you decide to test yourself through speed training and racing, you take certain risks, for a number of rewards. Speed training dramatically increases the chance of injury, aches and pains. As mentioned in a previous chapter, the quest toward a time goal can send the ego on a trip that reduces running enjoyment due to the narrow focus on a time goal. In this book there are suggestions for managing both of these potential problems—but you must be sensitive to the possibility of both.

The regular but gentle increase of speed repetitions stimulates the body to improve the efficiency of the mechanical workings of the feet, legs, and joints. The challenge of speed training also stimulates the inner workings of the muscle cells. The mitochondria, inner powerhouses that process energy, are pushed into delivering more, even when under duress. The individual muscle cells act as pumps, returning blood back to the heart and lungs. Even slow running, when done about 3 times a week, will help the mind and body work together, and strengthen the muscles for the type of running that you are doing. By testing yourself in speed sessions and races, you will be moving your "team" to a new level of performance.

## Getting faster requires extra work

To get faster, we must push beyond our current, comfortable levels. All of us have a lazy streak in us. Our bodies are programmed to conserve resources by doing the smallest amount of work they can get away with. So, even after we have increased the length of our runs steadily over several months, our leg muscles, tendons, ligaments etc. are not prepared for the jolt that speed training delivers. The best way to stay injury-free is to gradually increase the duration and intensity, eliminating the "jolt." But only when we put the legs, the heart, the lungs, etc., to a gentle test, week by week, does the body respond by improving in dozens of ways.

## Teamwork

When stressed, the heart, lungs, muscles, tendons, central nervous system, brain, and blood system are programmed to work as a team. The right brain intuitively solves problems, manages resources, and fine-tunes various processes mentioned above so that you can run faster.

## The long run builds endurance and a better plumbing system

By gradually extending slow long runs, you train muscle cells to expand their capacity to utilize oxygen efficiently, sustain energy production, and in general, increase capacity to go farther. The continued increase of the distance of long runs increases the reach of blood artery capillaries to deliver oxygen and an increased return of waste products, so that the muscles can work at top capacity. In short, long runs bestow a better plumbing system with greater muscle capacity. These changes will pay off when you do speed training.

## Endorphins kill pain, make you feel good

Running at about any pace, but especially speed training, signals to your body that there will be some pain to kill. The natural response is to produce natural pain killers called endorphins. These hormones act as drugs that relax and invigorate you with vitality, while bestowing a good attitude—even when tired after the run. If the rest interval is just right, you'll feel them kicking in-between faster segments of speed workouts.

## Gradually pushing up the workload

Your body is programmed to improve when it is gradually introduced to a little more work with enough rest afterward. Push too hard, or neglect the rest, and you'll see an increase in aches, pains, and injury. By balancing the speed workouts, adjusting for problems, and having realistic goals, most runners can continue to improve for several years.

## Stress + rest = improvement

When we run a little faster than our realistic goal pace, and increase the workload a little more than we did on last week's speed workout, this greater workload slightly breaks down the muscle cells, tendons, etc. just enough to stimulate change. You see, our bodies are programmed to rebuild stronger than before, but there must be gentle and regular stress, followed by significant rest to allow for the rebuilding to take place.

## Introducing the body to speed through 2 weeks of "drills"

As a gentle introduction to faster running, I've found nothing better than the two drills that are detailed in the "Drills" chapter: Turnover Drills & Acceleration-Gliders. The former helps to improve cadence of the legs and feet. The latter provides a very gentle introduction to speedwork, in very short segments.

Most of the running during the conditioning period is at an easy pace. These drills, done in the middle of a run, once or twice a week, will improve mechanics, get the muscles ready for the heavier demands of speed training, and initiate internal physiological changes in the muscles with very little risk of injury.

## A gentle increase in your weekly workouts causes a slight breakdown

The weekly speed workout starts with a few speed repetitions, with rest between each. As the number of repetitions increases each week, your body is pushed slightly beyond what it did the previous week. In each workout, your muscle fibers get tired as they reach the previous maximum workload, and continue like motivated slaves to keep you running the pace assigned. In every session some are pushed beyond their capacity with each additional speed repetition. Often, the pain and fatigue are not felt during the workout. But within one or two days there are usually sore muscles and tendons, and general overall tiredness. Even walking may not feel smooth for a day or two after a speed session.

## The damage

Looking inside the cell at the end of a hard workout, you'll see damage:

- There are tears in the muscle cell membrane.
- The mitochondria (that process the energy inside the cell) are swollen.
- There's a significant lowering of the muscle stores of glycogen (the energy supply needed in speedwork). Waste products from exertion, bits of bone and muscle tissue and other bio junk can be found.
- Sometimes, there are small tears in the blood vessels and arteries, and blood leaks into the muscles.

## The muscles rebound, stronger and better than before

Gentle overuse stimulates your body to not only repair the damage, but rebuild it stronger. The process puts the body organism on alert to be ready for more hard work, and to repair things better next time.

Two days after a speed session, if the muscles have had enough rest, you'll see some improvements:

- Waste has been removed.
- Thicker cell membranes can handle more work without breaking down.
- The mitochondria have increased in size and number, so that they can process more energy next time.
- The damage to the blood system has been repaired.
- Over several months, after adapting to a continued series of small increases, more capillaries (tiny fingers of the blood system) are produced, improving and expanding the delivery of oxygen and nutrients and providing a better withdrawal of waste products.

These are only some of the many adaptations made by the incredible human body when we exercise: bio-mechanics, nervous system, strength, muscle efficiency and more. Internal psychological improvements follow the physical ones. Mind, body, and spirit are becoming part of the process of improving health and performance. An added benefit is a positive attitude.

## Quality rest is crucial: 48 hours between workouts

Without sufficient rest, the damage won't be totally repaired. On rest days, it's important to avoid exercises that strenuously use the calf muscle, ankle and Achilles tendon (stair machines, step aerobics, spinning out of the saddle) for the 48 hour period between running workouts. If you have other aches and pains from your individual "weak links," then don't do exercises that aggravate them further. Walking is usually a great exercise for a rest day. There are several other good exercises in the "Cross Training" section of this book. As long as you are not continuing to stress the calf, most alternative exercises are fine.

## Beware of junk miles

Those training for a time goal often develop injuries because they try to "sneak in" a few miles on the days they should be resting. Even more than running long distance, speed training stresses the feet and legs and mandates the need for a 48 hour recovery period. The short, junk mile days don't help your conditioning, but they keep your muscles from recovering.

## Regularity

To maintain the adaptations, you must regularly run about every 2 days. To maintain the speed improvements mentioned in this book, you should do the speed workout once a week, every week. Waiting longer than this, will cause a slight loss in the capacity you have been developing each day. The longer you wait, the harder it will be to start up again. Staying regular with your exercise—and your speed training—is the best policy.

## "Muscle memory"

Your neuro-muscular system remembers the patterns of muscle activity which you have done regularly over an extended period of time. The longer you have been running regularly, the more easily it will be to start up when you've had a layoff. During your first few months of speedwork, for example, if you miss a weekly workout, you will need to drop back a week, and rebuild. But if you have run regularly for several years, and you miss a speed workout, little will be lost if you start the next one very slowly, and ease into it. Be careful as you return to speed training, if this happens.

## Tip: Cramped for time?
## Just do a few repetitions

Let's say that you cannot get to the track on your speed day, and you don't have but 15 minutes to run. Take a 3-4 minute slow warm-up with some accelerations, and do the same during the last 3-5 minutes. During the middle 5-9 minutes, run several 1-2 minute accelerations at approximately the pace you would run on the track. Don't worry if the pace is not perfect. Any of these segments is better than a week without any fast running at all.

## Aerobic running is done during long runs

*Aerobic* means "in the presence of oxygen." This is the type of running you do when you feel "slow" and comfortable. When running aerobically, your muscles can get enough oxygen from the blood to process the energy in the cells (burning fat in most cases). The minimal waste products produced during aerobic running can be easily removed, with no lingering build-up in the muscles.

## Speed training gets you into the anaerobic zone: an oxygen debt

*Anaerobic* running means running too fast or too long for you on that day. At some point in the workout, when you reach your current limit, the muscles can't get enough oxygen to burn the most efficient fuel, fat. So, they shift to the limited supply of stored sugar, glycogen. The waste products from this fuel pile up quickly in the cells, tightening the muscles and causing you to breathe heavily. This is called an oxygen debt. If you keep running for too long in this anaerobic state, you will have to slow down significantly or stop. But if you are running for a realistic time goal, and are pacing yourself correctly, you should only be running anaerobically for a short period of time at the end of each workout.

## The anaerobic threshold

As you increase the quantity of your speed sessions, you push back your anaerobic threshold. This means that you can run a bit farther than before—each week, at the same pace, without extreme huffing and puffing. Your muscles can move your body farther and faster without going to exhaustion. Each speed workout pushes you a little bit further into the anaerobic zone. Testing yourself means running with an oxygen debt. Speed training teaches the body and mind that they can go farther before going anaerobic, how to deal with the discomfort of this, and how to keep going when the muscles are tight and tired. It also tells you that you don't have to give up on performance when in this state. The process of coping with the stress of speedwork is the essence of running faster.

| You're aerobic— | if you can talk for as long as you want with minimal huffing & puffing (h & p) |
| --- | --- |
| You are mostly aerobic— | if you can talk for 30 sec + then must h & p for at least 10 sec |
| You are approaching anaerobic threshold— | if you can only talk for 10 seconds or less, then h & p for 10+ sec |
| You're anaerobic— | if you can't talk more than a few words, and are mostly huffing and puffing |

## Fast twitch vs. slow twitch muscle fibers

We are born with a combination of two types of muscle fibers. Those with a high percentage of fast twitchers can run fast for a short distance, and then become very tired. Fast twitch fibers are designed to burn the stored sugar in your muscles: glycogen. This is the fuel we use during the first 15 minutes of exercise, and it can produce a lot of waste products, such as lactic acid. If we run even a little too fast at the beginning of a run, the muscles will become very tight and tired very quickly, you will huff and puff, and feel increasingly uncomfortable.

If you have more slow twitch fibers, you won't be able to run as fast at first, but can keep going for longer distances.

Slow twitch fibers burn fat—a fuel that is very efficient and produces little waste product. Long runs will not only condition the slow twitch fibers to work to top capacity as they efficiently burn fat. As you increase the length of the long ones, you'll train some of your fast twitch fibers to burn fat as fuel.

Once the starting pace is controlled (and also the ego), fast runners develop a mix of fast and slow twitchers to do the work of running, and find that they don't get exhausted at the end. It is the slow pace and walk breaks that keep you in the aerobic zone, allowing you to push back the endurance limit.

## Mental changes—both positive and negative

When runners get more fit, their mental attitude changes in many positive ways. While self-confidence improves, a more positive attitude emerges. You'll deal better with stress, improve your general outlook on life, and have mental momentum for the stress of a time goal and other challenges in life.

### Are you working too hard on a time goal?

When runners get too focused on specific time goals they often find more stress and some negative attitude changes. At the first sign of these symptoms, back off and let mind and body get back together again.

- Running is not as enjoyable.
- You don't look forward to your runs.
- When you say something to others about your running, the statements are often negative.
- The negativity can permeate other areas of your life.
- You look on running as work instead of play.

## The personal growth of speed training

Instead of looking just at the times in your races, embrace the life lessons that can come from the journey of an extended speed training program. Most of your runs must have some fun in them to help you through this journey. Even after a hard workout, focus on how good you feel afterward, and on the satisfaction from meeting the challenge.

The reality of a speed training program is that you'll have more setbacks than victories. But, you will learn more from the setbacks and they will make you a stronger runner—and a stronger person. Confronting challenges is initially tough, but leads you to some of the great treasures of the improvement process. As you dig for deeper resources, you find that you have more strength inside than you thought—as you discover the path to them.

## Note

There's more on this topic in the "Mental Toughness" chapter.

# THE SIMPLE STRATEGY: GETTING FASTER... BY RUNNING FASTER

Marathon runners have known for decades that training for a shorter race will get the racing systems ready to run faster in the longer event. The same principle applies to those who want to run a faster 2 mile. The faster pace of both the workouts and the race itself forces the muscles, tendons, nerves, cardiovascular system, psyche, and spirit to gear up.

The regularity of the workouts set up a process of improving efficiency, as well as a system of searching for the resources needed to encounter challenges not faced before. For example, once you have trained to run faster, at the half mile distance, the pace for a one or two mile race seems easier. You also tend to feel smoother when you run this longer distance.

## Fact: running faster at a shorter distance can improve longer distance times

- To run a faster Marathon, you need to run faster in the 10K.
- To run a faster 10K, you need to run faster in the 5K.
- To run a faster 5K, you need to run faster in the mile, 2 mile or 1.5 mile.
- To run faster in the 1 and 2 mile distances, you need to run faster in the 800m.

## Training for the faster race stresses the system to improve

Each week, as you add to the work done in your speed workout, you slightly overwhelm the muscles and cardiovascular system. Your body has the incredible capacity to respond to this challenge by rebuilding stronger than before, with better efficiency.

## The faster speedwork produces systems that perform at a higher capacity

The faster pace of your speed workout coaxes adaptations out of the tendons, muscles, and the nerve system. You touch lighter, use your ankle and leg muscles more efficiently, while building the strength necessary to run faster.

## Sustained speed—through an increase in the number of repetitions

The maximum benefit from speed sessions is at the end of the program. As you increase the number of speed repetitions from 4 to 6, 8 and beyond, you teach yourself how to keep going at your assigned pace even when tired.

To maintain speed when tired is the mission. The only way to prepare for this "race reality" situation is to do this during speed training. Speedwork prepares you to keep on, keeping on when the legs usually would slow down.

## Longer runs maintain endurance—and improve your time

Your long runs will maintain or extend endurance, while you improve speed. Every week or two you'll run a very slow longer run. Many runners improve their times through this long run increase as much as, or more than from speed training. Both are important for maximum improvement.

## Running form improves

Regular speed workouts stimulate your body to run more efficiently. On each workout, as you push into fatigue, your body intuitively searches for ways of continuing to move at the same pace without extraneous motion: lighter touch of the feet, direct foot lift, lower to the ground, quicker turnover. See the "Running Form" chapter for more details.

## Watch out! Speedwork increases aches, pains and injuries

Speed training increases your chance of injury. Be sensitive to the areas on your foot, leg, muscles, etc., where you have had problems before. Think back to the patterns of aches and pains that have caused you to reduce or stop exercise in the past. You can reduce the chance of injury significantly by taking a day of two off at the flare-up of one of these, and by following the tips in the "Aches and Pains" chapter in this book.

# PREDICTING YOUR PERFORMANCE & MEASURING PROGRESS

*"The most important part of training for a goal is choosing one that is realistic."*

It's not enough to say that you are going to run a certain time in a race. If you are a very well-conditioned distance runner, and the goal is within your current capabilities, you may have performed at a higher level so many times that you may not need to write down your program of workouts. Most runners, however, will run faster, reduce aches and pains, and be more successful if they follow a successful plan. But the plan must be realistic.

By using a program that is based upon a realistic improvement strategy, you gain a significant amount of control over the improvement process. Through planning and a weekly test, you gain a vision of your fitness future, while preparing the mind for the challenge:

- A pre-test will tell you what goal is realistic.
- Weekly speed sessions develop the capacity to run faster.
- Weekly tests will tell you how you're doing, and set a realistic time to shoot for in the race itself.

You'll increase the potential for success greatly with a proven plan, improve your confidence, while you enjoy the satisfaction from being on a journey or mission that means something to you.

## Setting up your plan for success

1. Set the date or dates for your primary goal.

2. Run a pre-test to set your goal.

3. Use the prediction formula to see what you could run in your goal race right now.

4. Do a "leap of faith" improvement goal of up to 5%.

5. Set up your speed sessions based upon the "leap of faith" goal.

6. Do a weekly test race to monitor your progress.

7. As the primary goal race gets close, fine-tune your realistic goal by using the test races.

## Your goal race: the final exam

Once you have decided on your primary goal for this year, you've made the most important decision. Write this down in your calendar or journal. Even Marathoners can benefit from using the 5K program—but they must have enough time to insert this into their training calendar. Whatever the primary goal, you must first schedule the "big goal" (or all of them) in your training journal so that you can arrange workouts. This gives you a deadline around which you can schedule the other races and training elements which lead to it. If you tend to get sidetracked, you may need to keep reminding yourself throughout your journey that the final exam is the main goal, and your other races serve to evaluate the training as they improve your speed conditioning.

## If you don't have a final exam...

Some runners just like to receive regular feedback on how they are running. In this case, I suggest that you select a race at one or more strategic dates in your training as noted in the "Get a Journal" chapter in this book. It helps to schedule your efforts so that you can fine-tune your training and "test races" as you go through the program.

## Choose the distance of your "test races"

Your primary goal race will determine which test races you choose and then which training program you will use in this book.

| Primary mission | Test race distance |
| --- | --- |
| 5K | 1 mile |
| 2 mile | 800 meter |
| 1.5 mile | 800 meter |
| 1 mile | 800 meter |

## Conditioning background needed before starting this program

- At least 6 weeks of running and walking (if you don't have this, use the pre-season program below)
- A minimum of 3 days a week—for 30 min each day
- A long run of 3 miles (walk breaks included)
- Two weeks of acceleration-gliders, done during the middle of one run a week
- No injuries or ailments that would prevent strenuous, faster running

## Predicting race performance

During my competitive years and the first decade that I worked with other runners, I found a very beneficial prediction tool in *Computerized Running Training Programs* by Gerry Purdy and James Gardner. This book has been revised and re-published in print and software as *Running Trax*, by Track and Field News. This is a great resource and I highly recommend it.

The formula that I recommend to you is the result of over 3 decades of coaching, working with over 150,000 runners. For more detailed charts, see the resource above.

## Guidelines for using the formulas:

- You have done the training necessary for the goal—according to the training programs in this book.
- You are not injured.
- You run with an even-paced effort.
- The weather on race day is not adverse.

If your goal race does not produce the time predicted:

- Look at the pacing of your goal race—did you go too fast at the beginning?
- You may need a longer long run, or more speed repetitions.
- You may be tired going into the goal race.

## The pre-test

1. Go to a track, or another accurately measured course.
2. Warm up by walking for 5 minutes, then running a minute and walking a minute, then jogging an easy 800 meter (half mile or two laps around a track).
3. Do 4 acceleration-gliders. These are listed in the "Drills" chapter.
4. Walk for 3-4 minutes.
5. Run the distance of your test race—a hard effort.
6. On your first race, don't run all-out from the start—ease into your pace after the first third of the distance.
7. Warm down by reversing the warm-up.
8. A school track is the best venue. Don't use a treadmill because they tend to be notoriously un-calibrated, and often tell you that you ran farther or faster than you really did.
9. Use the table below to see how you are doing.

## To predict your time in a 1 mile, 1.5 mile, 2 mile:

Test race is 800 meters (two laps around a track)
This is a great race to chart progress in these distances. You should be able to run a hard 800 every week with no long term recovery issues. For an equivalent performance in the following distances, take out your calculator and do the math:

## Take your 800 meter time

| Goal race | Prediction formula |
|---|---|
| Mile | double the time, and add 35 seconds |
| 1.5 mile | multiply x 3 and add 60 seconds |
| 2 miles | multiply x 4 and add 1:30 |

Examples of equivalent performances by my formula:

| 800 time | Mile | 1.5 mile | 2 mile |
|---|---|---|---|
| 2:20 | 5:15 | 8:00 | 10:50 |
| 2:30 | 5:35 | 8:30 | 11:30 |
| 3:00 | 6:35 | 10:00 | 13:30 |
| 3:30 | 7:35 | 11:30 | 15:30 |
| 4:00 | 8:35 | 13:00 | 17:30 |
| 4:30 | 9:35 | 14:30 | 19:30 |
| 5:00 | 10:35 | 16:00 | 21:30 |
| 5:30 | 11:35 | 17:30 | 23:30 |
| 6:00 | 12:35 | 19:00 | 25:30 |
| 6:30 | 13:35 | 20:30 | 27:30 |
| 7:00 | 14:35 | 22:00 | 29:30 |
| 7:30 | 15:35 | 23:30 | 31:30 |
| 8:00 | 16:35 | 25:00 | 33:30 |
| 8:30 | 17:35 | 26:30 | 35:30 |
| 9:00 | 18:35 | 28:00 | 37:30 |
| 9:30 | 19:35 | 29:30 | 39:30 |
| 10:00 | 20:35 | 31:00 | 41:30 |

# To predict your 5K performance:

Test race 1 mile (4 laps around the track)

Take your one mile time and multiply by 3.1 then add 1:40

## Examples:

| One mile time | 5K prediction |
|---|---|
| 5:00 | 17:03 |
| 5:30 | 18:36 |
| 6:00 | 20:09 |
| 6:30 | 21:42 |
| 7:00 | 23:15 |
| 7:30 | 24:48 |
| 8:00 | 26:21 |
| 8:30 | 27:54 |
| 9:00 | 29:27 |
| 9:30 | 31:00 |
| 10:00 | 32:33 |
| 10:30 | 34:06 |
| 11:00 | 35:39 |
| 11:30 | 37:12 |
| 12:00 | 38:45 |
| 12:30 | 40:18 |
| 13:00 | 41:51 |
| 13:30 | 43:24 |

| One mile time | 5K prediction |
|---|---|
| 14:00 | 44:57 |
| 14:30 | 46:30 |
| 15:00 | 48:03 |
| 15:30 | 49:36 |
| 16:00 | 51:09 |
| 16:30 | 52:42 |
| 17:00 | 54:15 |
| 17:30 | 55:48 |
| 18:00 | 57:21 |
| 18:30 | 58:54 |
| 19:00 | 1:00:27 |
| 19:30 | 1:02:00 |
| 20:00 | 1:03:33 |

## The "leap of faith" goal prediction

It is OK to choose a time for your goal race which is faster than is predicted by your pre-test. As you do the speed training, the long runs and your test races, you should improve. For prediction purposes, as you take this "leap" to a goal, I suggest no more than a 3-5% improvement in a 3 month training program. Those who have a solid background of 2 years or more of running, but haven't done speed training for 1 year or more, can sometimes improve as much as 6-7%—although this is not common.

## How much of a "leap of faith"

| Pre-test prediction in the 2 mile | *3% Improvement | *5% Improvement |
|---|---|---|
| (Over a 2-3 month training program) | | |
| 40 minutes | 1 minute 12 sec | 2 minutes |
| 33 minutes | 60 seconds | 1 minute 40 seconds |
| 28 minutes | 50 seconds | 1 minute 24 seconds |
| 25 minutes | 45 seconds | 1 minute 15 seconds |
| 20 minutes | 36 seconds | 60 seconds |
| 17 minutes | 31 seconds | 51 seconds |
| 14 minutes | 25 seconds | 42 seconds |
| 12 minutes | 21 seconds | 36 seconds |

The key to goal setting is keeping your ego in check. From my experience, I have found that a 3% improvement is realistic. This means that if your 2 mile time is predicted to be 20 minutes, that it is realistic to assume that you could lower it by 36 seconds if you do the speed training and the long runs as noted on my training schedules a bit further in this book.

Those who have been running longer (two years or more) and have not been doing speed training for more than a year, could try for a more aggressive, 5% improvement: 1 minute off a 20 minute two mile race.

In all of these situations, however, everything must come together to produce the predicted result. You back up your goal prediction by doing the speedwork necessary for your goal. In the speed workouts, you'll run segments that are faster than your goal pace. Read the speed chapter and the training program chapters to see how this works.

## A weekly test

On one day each week, run your test distance as noted on the training schedule. This will help you chart your progress.

- Follow the same format as listed in the pre-test above.
- By doing this each week, you will get better at pacing yourself.
- Hint: it's better to start a bit more slowly than you think that you can run.
- Walk breaks will be helpful for most runners at a pace that is 10 min/mi or slower. Read the chapter on walk breaks to get suggestions.
- See how you're doing with each weekly test.
- If you are not making progress, then look for reasons and adjust.

## Reasons why you may not be improving:

1. You're over-trained, and tired—if so, reduce your training, and/or take an extra rest day.
2. You may have chosen a goal that is too ambitious for your current ability.
3. You may have missed some of your workouts, or not been as regular with your training.
4. The temperature may have been above 60°F (15°C). Above this, you will slow down.
5. When using different test courses, one of them may not have been accurately measured.

## Final reality check

The last two test races are crucial for predicting your race pace. Average the times from these two tests to get a good prediction in your goal race. It is possible to run faster than this prediction. It is strongly recommended that you run the first one-third of your goal race at the average pace, predicted by the last two races.

## Use a journal!

Read the chapter on using a journal. Your chance of reaching your goal increases greatly when you use this very important instrument. Psychologically, you start taking responsibility for the fulfillment of your mission when you use a journal.

# PRE-SEASON CONDITIONING

## Background needed before starting this program

- Walking, running or run-walking regularly for 3 weeks
- A minimum of 3 days a week—for 30 min each day
- No injuries or ailments that would prevent strenuous, faster running
- Be sure to tell your doctor that you want to do this training, and get his/her blessing before starting

# Note

The following is a training program for those who are starting from zero running. If you have been doing three months of regular but slow running, you could jump into the schedule at the amount of time you are running on the long run.

## Acceleration-gliders on Wednesday

In the 5th and 6th week you'll see the (A-G) notation. This is a drill that is inserted into the middle of your Wednesday run. You can read more about this in the "Drills" chapter of this book. These are very simple exercises which gradually introduce your muscles to faster running. Don't count the number of steps—this is only given as a general reference.

1. Jog very slowly for about 15 strides.
2. Jog faster for about 15 strides.
3. Over the next 15 strides, gradually increase pace. Don't come close to a sprint, just run faster than a fast jog. On each successive A-G, you could run just a little bit faster. Don't increase stride length much, if at all—use a quicker turnover of the feet and legs.
4. Then glide! The most effective part of the drill is training yourself how to use your momentum to glide or coast gradually down to a jog. At first you will only be able to do a few strides. If you do this once a week, you'll find yourself going farther on each "glide" after several weeks.
5. Repeat this 4-8 times.
6. To maintain your progress in this activity, do it every week. You can also do this drill on Monday if you wish.

# Note

Any time you increase your speed, you increase injury risk. You'll reduce this risk to minimal levels by gradually increasing speed, and being sensitive to all "weak link" areas that tend to get sore or painful when you run farther or faster than you have been running. When in doubt, don't run as fast, and provide more rest between runs.

## Pre-testing conditioning program

| Mon | Tues | Wed | Thu | Fri | Sa | Sun |
|---|---|---|---|---|---|---|
| **Week 1** | | | | | | |
| Walk 30 min | Walk 15 min | Walk 30 min | Walk 15 min | off | Walk 35 min | off |
| **Week 2** | | | | | | |
| 30 min run 10 sec/ walk 30 | Walk 30 min or off | 30 min run 10 sec/ walk 30 | Walk 30min or off | off | 40 min run 10 sec/ walk 30 | off |
| **Week 3** | | | | | | |
| 30 min run 15 sec /walk 30 | Walk 30 min or off | 30 min run 15 sec/ walk 30 | Walk 30 min or off | off | 45 min run 15 sec/ walk 30 | off |
| **Week 4** | | | | | | |
| 30 min run 20 sec/ walk 30 | Walk 30min or off | 30 min run 20 sec/ walk 30 | Walk 30min or off | off | 45-50 min run 20 sec/ walk 30 | off |

| Mon | Tues | Wed | Thu | Fri | Sa | Sun |
|-----|------|-----|-----|-----|-----|-----|
| **Week 5** | | | | | | |
| 30 min run 25 sec/ walk 30 | Walk 30min or off | 30 min (A-G) run 25 sec/ walk 30 | Walk 30min or off | off off | 45-55 min run 25 sec/ walk 30 | off |
| **Week 6** | | | | | | |
| 30 min run 30 sec/ walk 30 | Walk 30min or off | 30 min (A-G) run 30 sec/ walk 30 | Walk 30min or off | off off | 45-60 min run 30 sec/ walk 30 | off |

## Note

if you need several weeks at each run-walk ratio level, take it. This pre-conditioning training should not be stressful or painful. When in doubt, ease off.

# TRAINING PROGRAMS

**B**efore beginning the schedule below, you need to get your long run up to the distance of the first long one on the schedule. Your other runs should also be about 30 minutes or more, twice a week. For at least two weeks before the start of any of these programs, you should be running some acceleration/gliders (mentioned below) one day a week (not on a long run). It helps to have done the turnover drills for at least two weeks also. See the "Drills" chapter for simple instructions on how to do these.

## Every other day?

If you are already running more than 3 days a week, and are not experiencing any fatigue or injury issues, you can certainly continue with the number of days that work into your schedule. Be careful, however. Speed training, and the test days in this program will stress your muscles, tendons, motivation, etc. more than ever. When in doubt, back off and run the schedule below. If you are running more than three days a week, make sure that you take it very easy between each workout. I strongly suggest that you take a day off from running before the "test day" and before the speed workout day.

## Changing the specific workout days

It's fine to shift the days around, to accommodate your lifestyle. For example, you could run the long one on Sunday, take Monday off, and do the test day on Tuesday.

## How slow for the long runs—and how often the walk breaks

Long runs should be run at least 3 min/mi slower than your goal pace. Feel free to run slower than this.

## Examples:

| Goal pace (per mile) | Long run pace (per mile) |
|---|---|
| 5:00 | 8:00 |
| 6:00 | 9:00 |
| 7:00 | 10:00 |
| 8:00 | 11:00 |
| 9:00 | 12:00 |
| 11:00 | 14:00 |
| 13:00 | 16:00 |
| 15:00 | 18:00 |

## Walk breaks on long runs

Walk breaks can be taken according to the following schedule. Feel free to walk more or to cut both of the segments in half, for example: 1 min run/2 min walk could be converted to 30 seconds run/60 seconds walk.

| Pace of long run | # of min of running/# of minutes walking |
|---|---|
| 8:00 | 5 to 7 min run/1 min walk |
| 8:30 | 4-6 min run/1 min walk |
| 9:00 | 4-5/1 |
| 9:30 | 4-5/1 |
| 10:00 | 3-4/1 |
| 10:30 | 3-4/1 |
| 11:00 | 3/1 |
| 11:30 | 3/1 |
| 12:00 | 2-3/1 |
| 12:30 | 2-3/1 |
| 13:00 | 2/1 |
| 13:30 | 2/1 |
| 14:00 | 1-2/1 |
| 14:30 | 1-2/1 |
| 15:00 | 1/1 |
| 15:30 | 1/1 |
| 16:00 | 1/1.5 |
| 16:30 | 1/1.5 |
| 17:00 | 1/2 |
| 17:30 | 1/2 |
| 18:00 | 1 min run/2.5 min walk |
| 18:30 | 1 min run/2.5 min walk |
| 19:00 | 1 min run/3 min walk |
| 19:30 | 1 min run/3 min walk |
| 20:00 | 1 min run/3.5 min walk |

## Warm up (and warm down) before test days and speed day workouts

Here is a format that will get your mind and body ready to go faster. As you go through the training, fine-tune this to work for your specific needs. Then use the final product as your warm-up before the goal race.

The warm down should be a reversal of the warm-up. Never go from a fast repetition into the car or the shower. There is a cardiac risk in doing this.

1. Walk slowly for 5 minutes.
2. Run a minute and walk a minute for 10 minutes.
3. Jog slowly for 10 minutes.
4. Walk for 3-4 minutes.
5. Do a turnover drill (4-8 of them) see the "drill" chapter for details.
6. Walk for 1-3 minutes.
7. Do an acceleration-glider drill (4-8) see the "drill chapter for details.
8. Walk for 5 minutes.
9. Start the workout.

## Walk breaks in test races?

If you are running at 10 min/mi or slower you will benefit from a short walk break every lap or two when the race distance is one mile or more. Many runners down to a 8 min/mi pace have told me that they benefit from the short walks. At the 800 meter distance, runners who are running at a 12 min pace or slower per mile can often benefit from a 10-15 second walk break at the half way point. The following are suggestions, but you will need to find the ratio that works best for you.

| Pace of race (per mile) | # of seconds walking |
|---|---|
| 8:00 | 10-15 sec every 3 laps |
| 8:30 | 10-15 sec every 2 laps |
| 9:00 | 12-18 sec every 2 laps |
| 9:30 | 15-20 sec every 2 laps |
| 10:00 | 7-10 sec every lap |
| 10:30 | 8-12 sec every lap |
| 11:00 | 9-13 sec every lap |
| 11:30 | 10-15 sec every lap |
| 12:00 | 11-16 sec every lap |
| 12:30 | 12-17 sec every lap |
| 13:00 | 13-18 sec every lap |
| 13:30 | 14-19 sec every lap |
| 14:00 | 15-20 sec every lap |
| 14:30 | 16-21 sec every lap |
| 15:00 | 17-22 sec every lap |
| 15:30 | 18-23 sec every lap |
| 16:00 | 19-24 sec every lap |
| 16:30 | 10-11 sec every half lap |
| 17:00 | 11-12 sec every half lap |
| 17:30 | 12-13 sec every half lap |
| 18:00 | 13-14 sec every half lap |
| 18:30 | 14-15 sec every half lap |
| 19:00 | 15-16 sec every half lap |
| 19:30 | 16-17 sec every half lap |
| 20:00 | 17-18 sec every half lap |

# Test races

These are the "reality checks" on your goal. Every other week you will run a timed race at 800m or 1 mile. You may take walk breaks or not on these time trials, it's your choice. With each of these test races, your goal is to run closer and closer to a maximum effort at the short distance. After you run each race, go to the prediction formula in the earlier chapter in this book, and compute the equivalent time in your goal race.

If your predictions are a few seconds off what you want to run in your goal race, it's OK to continue to train for your original goal. In the goal race, a safe strategy is to start the race at the pace that you are predicting as an average of your last two races.

If your predicted time at the end of the program is still 30 seconds or more slower than your goal pace, start your race at the time predicted by the test races. If you have something left (and this often happens), go for the goal at the half way point in the goal race.

## Test race workouts (WO)

The workouts listed on test days will prepare you for your race. The first segment should be run as close as you can to the race pace, lap by lap. Walk for at least 5 minutes (no more than 10 minutes) and then do the second segment, trying to run about 1-2 seconds per lap faster than the goal pace. Each lap on a standard track is 400 meters.

## Speed days

Each of these 400 meter laps should be run 5-7 seconds faster than you want to run a 400 ( = .25 mile). Walk for 2-3 minutes and repeat the process. In other words, take the per mile pace you want to run in your goal race, divide it by 4, and subtract 5-7 seconds. Example: your goal pace is 8 minutes per mile. Eight divided by 4 = 2 minutes. Subtracting 7 seconds means that your workout pace per lap is 1:53.

# Note

Even experienced runners increase injury risk when they incorporate speed training. Be sensitive to all "weak link" areas and cut back according to the injury section of the book.

| | |
|---|---|
| WO = | *workout* |
| * = | *cadence drill* |
| ** = | *acceleration gliders* |
| XT = | *cross training* |

## 1 mile training program

| Mon | Tues | Wed | Thu | Fri | Sat | Sun |
|---|---|---|---|---|---|---|
| **Week 1** | | | | | | |
| Test day */**800m | Walk 30 min or XT or off | Speed day */**4x400m | Walk 30 min or XT or off | off | Long run 3 mi easy | off |
| **Week 2** | | | | | | |
| Test day (WO) 1000m/ race pace (*/ **) | Walk 30 min or XT or off | Speed Day 5x400m (*/ **) | Walk 30 min or XT or off | off | Long run 3.5 mi or off | off |

| Mon | Tues | Wed | Thu | Fri | Sat | Sun |
|---|---|---|---|---|---|---|
| **Week 3** | | | | | | |
| Test day */**800m | Walk 30 min or XT or off | Speed day */**6x400m | Walk 30 min or XT or off | off | Long run 4 mi | off |
| **Week 4** | | | | | | |
| Test day (WO) 1200m/ race pace (*/ **) | Walk 30 min or XT or off | Speed day 7x400m (*/ **) | Walk 30 min or XT or off | off | Long run 4.5 mi | off |
| **Week 5** | | | | | | |
| Test day */**800m | Walk 30 min or XT or off | Speed day */**8x400m | Walk 30 min or XT or off | off | Long run 5 mi | off |
| **Week 6** | | | | | | |
| Test day (WO) 1200m/ race pace plus 600 meter (*/**) | Walk 30 min or XT or off | Speed day 8-9x400m (*/**) | Walk 30 min or XT or off | off | Long run 5 mi | off |
| **Next week:  Goal Race** | | | | | | |
| 3-4x400m at race pace walk 3-4 min between ea (*/**) | XT or off | 3-4x400m at race pace walk 3-4 min between ea (*/**) | XT or off | Goal race | XT or off | |

# 1.5 mile training program

| Mon | Tues | Wed | Thu | Fri | Sat | Sun |
|---|---|---|---|---|---|---|
| **Week 1** | | | | | | |
| Test day */**800m | Walk 30 min or XT or off | Speed day */**5x400m | Walk 30 min or XT or off | off | Long run 3.5 mi | off |
| **Week 2** | | | | | | |
| Test day (WO) 1200m/ race pace plus 400m (*/**) | Walk 30 min or XT or off | Speed day 6x400m (*/**) | Walk 30 min or XT or off | off | Long run 4 mi | off |
| **Week 3** | | | | | | |
| Test day */**800m | Walk 30 min or XT or off | Speed day */**7x400m | Walk 30 min or XT or off | off | Long run 4.5 mi | off |
| **Week 4** | | | | | | |
| Test day (WO) 1200m/ race pace plus 800m (*/**) | Walk 30 min or XT or off | Speed day 8x400m (*/**) | Walk 30 min or XT or off | off | Long run 5.0 mi | off |
| **Week 5** | | | | | | |
| Test day */**800m | Walk 30 min or XT or off | Speed day */**9x400m | Walk 30 min or XT or off | off | Long run 5.5 mi | off |

| Mon | Tues | Wed | Thu | Fri | Sat | Sun |
|---|---|---|---|---|---|---|
| **Week 6** | | | | | | |
| Test day (WO) 1mi/ race pace plus 800m (*/**) | Walk 30 min or XT or off | Speed day 10x400m (*/**) | Walk 30 min or XT or off | off | Long run 6 mi | off |
| **Next week:  Goal Race** | | | | | | |
| 3-4x400m at race pace walk 3-4 min between ea (*/**) | XT or off or walk | 3-4x400m at race pace walk 3-4 min between ea (*/**) | XT or off | off | Goal race | off |

# 2 mile

| Mon | Tues | Wed | Thu | Fri | Sat | Sun |
|-----|------|-----|-----|-----|-----|-----|
| **Week 1** | | | | | | |
| Test day */**800m | Walk 30 min or XT or off | Speed day */**6x400m | Walk 30 min or XT or off | off | Long run 4 mi | off |
| **Week 2** | | | | | | |
| Test day (WO)1mi/ race pace plus 400m (*/**) | Walk 30 min or XT or off | Speed day 7x400m (*/**) | Walk 30 min or XT or off | off | Long run 4.5 mi | off |
| **Week 3** | | | | | | |
| Test day */**800m | Walk 30 min or XT or off | Speed day */**8x400m | Walk 30 min or XT or off | off | Long run 5 mi | off |
| **Week 4** | | | | | | |
| Test day (WO) 1.25 mi/ race pace plus 800m (*/**) | Walk 30 min or XT or off | Speed day 9x400m (*/**) | Walk 30 min or XT or off | off | Long run 5.5 mi | off |
| **Week 5** | | | | | | |
| Test day */**800m | Walk 30 min or XT or off | Speed day */**10x400m | Walk 30 min or XT or off | off | Long run 6 mi | off |

| Mon | Tues | Wed | Thu | Fri | Sat | Sun |
|-----|------|-----|-----|-----|-----|-----|

| | | | | | | |
|-----|------|-----|-----|-----|-----|-----|
| **Week 6** | | | | | | |

| Mon | Tues | Wed | Thu | Fri | Sat | Sun |
|-----|------|-----|-----|-----|-----|-----|
| Test day (WO) 1.5/ race pace plus 800m (*/**) | Walk 30 min or XT or off | Speed day 11x400m (*/**) | Walk 30 min or XT or off | off | Long run 6-6.5 mi | off |

| | | | | | | |
|-----|------|-----|-----|-----|-----|-----|
| **Next week: Goal Race** | | | | | | |

| Mon | Tues | Wed | Thu | Fri | Sat | Sun |
|-----|------|-----|-----|-----|-----|-----|
| 3-4x400m at race pace walk 3-4 min between ea (*/**) | XT or off | 3-4x400m at race pace walk 3-4 min between ea (*/**) | XT or off | | Goal race | XT or off |

# 5K

| Mon | Tues | Wed | Thu | Fri | Sat | Sun |
|-----|------|-----|-----|-----|-----|-----|
| **Week 1** | | | | | | |
| Test day (*/**)1 mi | Walk 30 min or XT or off | Speed day */**6x400m | Walk 30 min or XT or off | off | Long run 5 mi | off |
| **Week 2** | | | | | | |
| Test day (WO) 1.5mi race pace plus 1200m (*/**) | Walk 30 min or XT or off | Speed day 8x400m (*/**) | Walk 30 min or XT or off | off | Long run 6 mi | off |
| **Week 3** | | | | | | |
| Test day */**1 mi | Walk 30 min or XT or off | Speed day */**10x400m | Walk 30 min or XT or off | off | Long run 7 mi | off |
| **Week 4** | | | | | | |
| Test day (WO) 2 mi race pace plus 800m (*/**) | Walk 30 min or XT or off | Speed day 12x400m (*/**) | Walk 30 min or XT or off | off | Long run 8 mi | off |
| **Week 5** | | | | | | |
| Test day */**1 mi | Walk 30 min or XT or off | Speed day */**13x400m | Walk 30 min or XT or off | off | Long run 9 mi | off |

| Mon | Tues | Wed | Thu | Fri | Sat | Sun |
|---|---|---|---|---|---|---|
| **Week 6** | | | | | | |
| Test day (WO) 2.25mi/ race pace plus 1200m (*/**) | Walk 30 min or XT or off | Speed day 14x400m (*/**) | Walk 30 min or XT or off | off | Long run 10 mi | off |
| **Next week: Goal Race** | | | | | | |
| 3-4x400m at race pace walk 3-4 min between ea (*/**) | XT or off | 3-4x400m | XT or off at race pace walk 3-4 min between ea (*/**) | | Goal race | off |

# THE DRILLS TO MAKE RUNNING FASTER AND EASIER

The following drills have helped thousands of runners run more efficiently and faster. Each works toward a slightly different goal, but all of them reward the individual for pulling together the various running form components to eliminate extraneous motion in your feet and legs, reduce impact, use momentum, and increase the cadence or turnover of your feet and legs. Each month you will be teaching yourself to run more directly and efficiently.

# When?

These should be done on a non-long run day. It is fine, however, to do them as part of your warm-up, before a race or a speed workout. Many runners have also told me that the drills are a nice way to break up an average run that they sometimes call "boring."

## Cadence or turnover drill

This is an easy drill that improves the efficiency of running, making running easier. This drill excels in how it helps to pull all the elements of good running form together at the same time. Over the weeks and months, if you do this drill once every week, you will find that your normal cadence slowly increases naturally.

1. Warm up by walking for 5 minutes, and running and walking very gently for 10 minutes.
2. Start jogging slowly for 1-2 minutes, and then time yourself for 30 seconds. During this half minute, count the number of times your left foot touches.
3. Walk around for a minute or so.
4. On the 2nd 30 second drill, increase the count by 1 or 2.
5. Repeat this 3-7 more times. Each time trying to increase by 1-2 additional counts.

In the process of improving turnover, the body's internal monitoring system, coordinates a series of adaptations which makes the feet, legs, nerve system and timing mechanism work together as an efficient team:

- Your foot touches more gently.
- Extra, inefficient motions of the foot and leg are reduced or eliminated.
- Less effort is spent on pushing up or moving forward.

- You stay lower to the ground.
- The ankle becomes more efficient.
- Ache and pain areas are not overused.

## Acceleration-glider drills

This drill is a form of speed play, or fartlek. By doing it regularly, you develop a range of speeds with the muscle conditioning to move smoothly from one to the next. The greatest benefit comes as you learn how to "glide", or coast off your momentum.

1. Done on a non-long-run day, in the middle of a shorter run, or as a warm-up for a speed session or a race or test day.
2. Warm up with at least half a mile of easy running.
3. Many runners do the turnover drill just after the easy warm-up, and then do the acceleration-gliders. But these can be done separately from the turnover drill if desired.
4. Run 4-8 of them.
5. Do this at least once a week.
6. No sprinting—never run all-out.

After teaching this drill at my one-day running schools and weekend retreats for years, I can say that most people learn better through practice when they work on the concepts listed below—rather than the details of the drill. So just get out there and try them!

*Gliding*—The most important concept. This is like coasting off the momentum of a downhill run. You can do some of your gliders running down a hill if you want, but it is important to do at least two of them on the flat land.

*Do this every week*—As in the turnover drills, the regularity of the drill is very important. If you're like most runners, you won't glide very far at first. Regular practice will help you glide farther and farther.

*Don't sweat the small stuff*—I've included a general guideline of how many steps to do with each part of the drill, but don't worry about getting any exact number of steps. It's best to get into a flow with this drill and not worry at all about how many steps you are taking.

*Smooth transition*—between each of the components. Each time you "shift gears" you are using the momentum of the current mode to start you into the next mode. Don't make a sudden and abrupt change, but have a smooth transition between modes.

Here's how it's done:

- Start by jogging very slowly for about 15 steps.
- Then, jog faster for about 15 steps—increasing to a regular running pace for you.
- Now, over the next 15 steps, gradually increase the speed to your current race pace.
- OK, it's time to glide, or coast. Allow yourself to gradually slow down to a jog using momentum as long as you can. At first you may only glide for 4 or 5 steps. As the months go by, you will get up to 20, then 30 and beyond....you're gliding!

*Overall Purpose:* As you do this drill, every week, you will feel smoother at each mode of running. Congratulations! You are learning how to keep moving at a fairly fast pace without using much energy. This is the main object of the drill.

There will be some weeks when you will glide longer than others—don't worry about this. By doing this drill regularly, you will find yourself coasting or gliding down the smallest of inclines, and even for 10-20 yards on the flat on a regular basis. Gliding conserves energy reduces soreness, fatigue, and maintains a faster pace in races.

# GET A JOURNAL AND USE IT!

*"A journal allows you to take charge of your running future."*

A journal will help you chart your progress, and fine-tune it for more efficient goal pursuit. You'll be motivated as you log your runs. When things aren't going well, you can often find the reasons in your journal. As you get better at recording the "little things," you will have a gold mine of information and very possibly pick out the early warning signs of overuse.

By scheduling ahead, you can arrange the workouts (and rest) in your training program, so that you can train more consistently and effectively to your goal. As you preview 2-3 weeks ahead, you can adjust the training based upon your recovery. When you notice the symptoms of fatigue, schedule more rest. In this way the journal helps you avoid over-training and injury, while you adjust the workouts that you need for your goals.

Veterans: Sometimes advanced runners feel that they don't need to keep a journal. I've found, however, that when runners are approaching a goal that is really challenging, the journal brings a sense of confidence and a sense of focus. Journals allow time goal runners at all levels to fine-tune the little things that result in those few seconds of improvement— the crucial seconds that make it all worthwhile.

Beginners: Those who start their journal when they begin to do speedwork for the first time can see dramatic progress in a month or two. Beginners should look over the "conditioning schedule" or the appropriate training schedule, and start writing!

## The various types of journals

### Calendar
This is the first journal used by many runners. Posted on the wall or the refrigerator, you can jot down each day's total with a few notes.

### An organized training journal
The products that are designed for running make the recording of information much easier—you don't have to think. If the items you need are not printed, add them. My

*Jeff Galloway's Training Journal* has log pages with training information.

### Notebook
Just go to a drugstore or office supply store and get a school notebook. The blank pages invite you to write what is important to you.

### Computer logs
A growing number of software products allow you to sort through information more quickly. In working with a company (PC Coach) to incorporate my training program, I discovered that this format speeds up the search for information you need. For those who enjoy working with computers and software products, this is a great journal format. The PC coach software allows for pace download from several watches and heart monitors.

### What to record in the journal
Right after the run, quickly jot down a few details. If you do this regularly, you'll get really good at recording a lot of info in a short amount of time. If you have to think about an item, skip it and just fill in the items you can quickly. Here is a list of commonly recorded data, but insert your own items.

## TIP

Many speed-trained runners write the speed workouts in a bright color for quick recognition. If you don't see the bright print, and the week is almost over, you know that you need to get to the track!

## Basic components

Date:

Morning pulse (see sidebar below)

Time of run:

Distance covered:

Time running:

Pace per mile:

Weather:

Temperature:

Precipitation:

Humidity:

## Speed components

# of repetitions:

Pace of each:

Rest interval:

Warm-up/warm down:

Aches, pains, etc:

## Comments:

Walk-Run frequency:

Any notable aspect of the workout:

Running companion:

Terrain:

How did you feel (1-10):

*The "little things"*

Look over your entries, and add some comments. If your ankle hurt in the middle of the workout, make a note, even if you think it may not be important. Be sensitive to your weak links. Write down any unusual reaction of the body during or after the workout. Fill in the details! These will help you track down causes of future problems so that you can avoid them in the future. You're also authorized to read back over the workouts that led to your successes—and gloat!

## Scheduling the elements

Now it's time to schedule your workouts, week by week. Open up your journal and start writing down each of the items below. I suggest that you use the priorities listed below—but make the program work for your lifestyle and goals.

• *First priority: Goal race or races*
  Write down your primary goal race (or races) in your journal on the days they will occur. This will provide the focal point of the training program. As you fill in the pages leading up to this date, you will schedule the other elements, and then write down what you actually did.

• *If you don't have a goal race*
  Look ahead in the year and schedule a race or two that will give you a "date on a calendar." Even if you don't feel compelled to run a personal record, you will have an "anchor" to the program, so that your earlier races lead to a conclusion. For example, you could stage gradually increasing race distances: 800m, 1 mile, 2 mile, and finish with a 5K—over a 2-3 month period.

- *Write down your long runs*

  Each weekend in your journal, write down the projected long runs, from the goal race date backwards. The long runs will give you more conditioning value than any other component of the program, but can cause problems when run too fast. Be sure to record pace, outdoor temperature during the run, aches and pains, etc.

- *Schedule your test races*

  Based upon your goal race, choose either 800m, 1 mile, 2 mile, or 5K as your "test race distance." On each "test race Monday," as you run these, note your time for each, the weather, and any other facts that can seem unusual: aches, pacing, shoe problems, stomach issues, etc.

| Test race | Goal race |
|---|---|
| 800m | 1 mile, 1.5 mile, or 2 mile |
| 1 mile or 2 mile | 5K or 10K |
| 5K | marathon or half marathon |

- *Schedule the workouts needed for your goal race*

  Take the schedule of workouts, listed in the "Training Program" chapter, and write them into your training journal on the dates they should be run. As you record the results, note the same items mentioned in the test race segment just above.

- *Fill in all of the other runs*

  For most runners, an every-other-day running program is best. This allows time for the running muscles to recover. Look over your training schedule, so that you have the right balance between running days and rest days—for you. The journal gives you the chance to plan ahead for scenic runs, social jogs, etc.

- *Fine-tune*
  Each day, before your run, look at your journal. Peek ahead at the next few runs. Look back to remind yourself of problems during the last runs, or adjustments that you may need to make. As you make these modifications, your journal becomes part of you, and you head in the direction of your goal.

# THE GALLOWAY RUN-WALK METHOD

*"It is hard to believe, but thousands of runners have improved their times by taking walk breaks."*

Running continuously causes the muscles to fatigue more rapidly, primarily because the muscles must be used lap after lap, or mile after mile—without relief. If you break the cycle of continuous use by walking early enough, you allow the muscles to rebound, so that they can go farther or faster at the end. This process gives you an extraordinary degree of control over the amount of fatigue you put on your legs.

## Walk before you get tired

If you want to have leg strength at the end, you need to take walk breaks from the beginning—before you start to get tired. With each walk in the first third of the run, you increase bounce of your muscles at the end as you decrease the leg fatigue. The most important walk break is the first one. Many runners have trouble with this and don't walk until they're tired. As a result, they have trouble starting back up from their break.

## You can control your fatigue!

By using a ratio of running and walking that works for you, you'll conserve energy, keep the muscles resilient and strong, and recover fast. Having a strategy that works so well, bestows a mental confidence which will help you later in a challenging run. After long training runs, you want to recover fast, so that you can get on to your other training. Walk breaks speed recovery faster than anything I've found. There is no need to reach the end of a long run, feeling exhausted—your legs stay fresh by taking liberal walk breaks.

## Walk breaks....

- give you control over your level of strength at the end of a run
- erase fatigue
- push back your fatigue wall
- allow for endorphins to collect during each walk break—you feel good!
- break up the distance into manageable units ("one more minute")
- speed up the recovery of your leg muscles
- reduce the chance of aches, pains and injury

- allow you to feel good afterward—carrying on the rest of your day without debilitating fatigue
- give you all of the speed or endurance of each session—without the pain
- allow older runners to recover fast, and feel as good or better than the younger days
- help you run faster by not slowing down at the end of races!

## A short but quick walking stride

It's better to walk with a short stride. There has been some irritation of the shins when runners or walkers maintain a stride that is too long. Through practice, you can increase the pace of your walk as you develop a smooth, quick stride through quick turnover.

## Personal endorsement

After 50 years of running, I enjoy running more than ever today, because of walk breaks. Each walk I take energizes my run. Because I walk early and often, I've increased my frequency of running to almost every day. I start most runs taking a short walk break every minute. By 2 miles I am usually walking every 3-4 minutes. By 5 miles the ratio often goes to every 7-10 minutes. But there are days every year when I stay at 3 minutes and even a few days at 1 min. Even in races, I take short walks on hills and at water stations, and find that I have much more bounce in the legs than when I try to run continuously.

## A long run with walk breaks gives you the same endurance

On long runs, the distance is the only thing that matters. You get the same endurance whether you take walk breaks or not.

*Your choice:*

- A long run of 5 miles run continuously gives 5 miles of endurance.

- A long run with walk breaks gives 5 miles of endurance, but allows for much quicker recovery, and more enjoyment.

## Running continuously can compromise a time goal

Runners who do not take walk breaks risk not fully recovering from the long run. The residual fatigue is carried into the speed sessions, and compounded by other long runs.

As the lingering fatigue builds up, tired muscles can't deliver the performance in the race that they could have done with walk breaks.

## How to use walk breaks on long runs

1. Look at the schedule below as a guide (you can take them more often with no penalty).
2. Be sure to take the walk breaks from the beginning.
3. When in doubt, take the walk breaks more often.

## How to pace the long runs

1. Run a one mile time trial—4 laps around a standard 400 meter track.
2. Long runs should be paced at least 3 min/mi slower than your one mile pace.
3. Take walk breaks according to the schedule below (or more often).

| | |
|---|---|
| 7 min mile: | 7 min run—1 min walk |
| 8 min mile: | 5-6 min run—1 min walk |
| 9 min mile: | 4-5 min run—1 min walk |
| 10 min mile: | 3-4 min run—1 min walk |
| 11 min mile: | 2-3 min run—1 min walk |
| 12 min mile: | 2 min run—1 min walk |
| 13 min mile: | 1-2 min run—1 min walk |
| 14 min mile: | 1-2 min run—1 min walk |
| 15 min mile: | 1 min run—1 min walk |
| 16 min mile: | 30 seconds run—30 seconds walk |
| 17 min mile: | 30 seconds run—30-60 seconds walk |
| 18 min mile: | 30 seconds run—60 seconds walk |
| 19 min mile: | 20-30 seconds run—60 seconds walk |
| 20 min mile: | 20 seconds run—60 seconds walk |

## How to keep track of the walk breaks

There are various brands of watches which can be set to "beep" when it's time to walk, and then "beep" again when it's time to start running again. Check our website (www.jeffgalloway.com) or a good running store for advice in this area.

## Walk breaks in races?

Each year I hear from a growing number of runners who run faster when they add short walk breaks during their race. If you are running at 8 min/mi or slower you will probably benefit from a short walk break every lap or two when the race distance is one mile or more. After the half way point in your goal race, you can run continuously to the finish or reduce the walk breaks—your choice.

Even at the 800 meter distance, runners who are running at a 12 min pace or slower per mile can often benefit from a short walk break, as noted on the schedule below. The following are suggestions, but you will need to find the ratio that works best for you. Practice this on your Monday time trial workouts (the Mondays when you are not doing a test race), and go with the ratio and frequency that works best.

| Pace of the race/per mi | # of seconds walking |
| --- | --- |
| 8:00 | 5-10 sec every 2 laps |
| 8:30 | 8-12 sec every 2 laps |
| 9:00 | 10-15 sec every 2 laps |
| 9:30 | 12-18 sec every 2 laps |
| 10:00 | 5-8 sec every lap |
| 10:30 | 7-10 sec every lap |
| 11:00 | 9-12 sec every lap |
| 11:30 | 10-15 sec every lap |
| 12:00 | 11-16 sec every lap |
| 12:30 | 12-17 sec every lap |
| 13:00 | 13-18 sec every lap |
| 13:30 | 14-19 sec every lap |
| 14:00 | 15-20 sec every lap |
| 14:30 | 16-21 sec every lap |
| 15:00 | 17-22 sec every lap |
| 15:30 | 18-23 sec every lap |
| 16:00 | 19-24 sec every lap |
| 16:30 | 10-11 sec every half lap |
| 17:00 | 11-12 sec every half lap |
| 17:30 | 12-13 sec every half lap |
| 18:00 | 13-14 sec every half lap |
| 18:30 | 14-15 sec every half lap |
| 19:00 | 15-16 sec every half lap |
| 19:30 | 16-17 sec every half lap |
| 20:00 | 17-18 sec every half lap |

*"Don't be afraid to experiment with walk breaks"*

# RACING INJURY FREE

*"The single greatest reason for improvement in running is not getting injured."*

This chapter is dedicated to setting up a systematic training plan that has kept thousands of runners injury-free, for years. Also included, at no additional cost, is an injury action plan should you slip into the "injury zone."

Before I followed the suggestions below, I had hundreds of injuries. I am so proud to tell you that due mainly to prevention and quick treatment, I've haven't had a single overuse injury in over 25 years. I pass on what I've learned as one runner to another. For medical advice, be sure to see a doctor.

## Balancing your mental focus—to stay away from injury

Everyone knows that you need to increase the intensity of your speed training to stimulate improvement. The problem is deciding how to do this, and how much rest between hard workouts. I hear from a lot of injured runners. After many interviews, I've discovered that most are doing the big things right. The injuries often sneak up through a series of little mistakes. When you're focused and motivated, it is too easy to push just a little too hard, neglect rest, and start back just a little too soon before healing has taken place. For lots more information on this, read the "What Happens Inside Us..." chapter in this book—and *Galloway's Book on Running*.

## Strategic rest is even more important for time goal runners

Running at any speed produces a number of micro tears in the muscle cell and tendons. The harder you run, or the more speed repetitions you accumulate, the more damage. By the time you reach the last third of your time improvement program, strategic rest is a little more important than the speed workouts. You still need to do the workouts. But a high percentage of the speed-related injuries occur in the few weeks before a goal race. Very often just one extra day of rest between speed sessions, at the first sign of a possible injury, could have repaired the damage. The lesson: when in doubt, take an extra day off from running.

But inside each human is a personality trait that can compromise running enjoyment. I call this the "type A speed syndrome." Even those who feel they have no competitive urges and no athletic background need to be on guard. Once a new runner has achieved a certain level of fitness, there is a tendency to push more or rest less. At first, the body responds. When the runner keeps pushing, at some point the body breaks at one of the "weak links." The good news is that we usually receive an early warning sign or two.

## Be sensitive to weak links: in the knee, foot, ankle, shin, hip...

Unique to each of us are a few body parts and connections that take on more stress. You'll get to know these areas, because most of the aches, pains, and injuries will occur there. Most commonly, the sites are the knees, the foot, the shins, and the hip. You probably know most of your weak links already, so you need to be very sensitive to aggravation and/or pain in these areas.

## Little mistakes that cause big injuries

- Running only 2 more repetitions when there is inflammation, etc.
- Running one more mile at the end of a long run, when the foot, etc., is not working correctly
- The knee, etc., still hurts, so you just do a short and easy run (instead of taking the day off)

## Is it an injury?

The following are the "red flags" that could indicate an injury. At the first sign of any of the below, stop your workout immediately and take some extra rest days (usually 2-3). Running at the early stages of an injury creates a dramatically worse injury—even on one run—especially when you're running speedwork or races. If you take

2-3 days off at the first symptom, you may avoid having to stop exercise for 2-3 weeks or months by continuing to run. It is always better to err on the side of taking more time off.

1. **Inflammation**—any type of swelling

2. **Loss of function**—the foot, etc, doesn't work the way it usually does

3. **Pain**—that does not go away when you walk for a few minutes

## Losing conditioning?

Don't worry about losing your conditioning, even if you have to stop running for 5 days. In most cases, one or two extra days off are all that is needed. Most mistakes are made during the first few days of an injury when you just don't want to lose training time. Remember that staying injury free has an even higher priority: you will run slower and slower when injured. So don't be afraid to take up to 5 days off when a "weak link" kicks in. In most cases you will only need to stop for 2 days. But if it takes more time to heal than 5 days—let it heal!

## Treatment

It is always best, at the first sign of injury, to see a doctor (or with muscle injury, a massage therapist) who wants to get you out there running as soon as possible. Try to find one that has worked with many track athletes, or lots of runners. The better doctors will explain what they believe is wrong (or tell you when he/she cannot come up with a diagnosis) and give you a treatment plan. If you have confidence in the doctor, you will tend to follow the advice. This set of conditions has been shown to speed the healing.

## Treatments while you are waiting to see a doctor

Unfortunately, you may have to wait to get an appointment with one of the better doctors. While waiting for your appointment, here are some things other runners have done to speed up healing of an aggravated "weak link."

1. Take at least 2-5 days off from any activity that could irritate it.

2. If the area is next to the skin (tendon, foot, etc.), rub a chunk of ice on the area(s)—constantly rubbing for 15 min each night until the area gets numb. Continue to do this for a week after you feel no symptoms.

3. If the problem is inside a joint or muscle, call your doctor's office and ask the nurse or medical assistant if you can use prescription strength anti-inflammatory medication. Don't take any medication without a doctor's advice—and follow that advice.

4. Even if the injury is healed enough to run, you should avoid doing speed training for at least a week after the pain has gone away.

5. If you have a muscle injury, see a very successful sports massage therapist. Try to find one who has a lot of successful experience treating the type of muscle group that is injured. The magic fingers and hands can often work wonders.

Many runners assume that any frozen item can be used in an ice treatment, and use plastic bags of ice, frozen ice gel, even frozen bags of peas. In my experience, these forms of ice treatment do no good at all. When ice is rubbed directly on the skin, as noted below, it is a very powerful treatment for aches, pains and injuries that are just below the skin. Deeper damage does not usually respond to the ice treatment.

- Put a styrofoam cup full of water, in your freezer. Keep at least one there, as "insurance."

- At the first sign of an ache or pain in an area close to the skin, peel the styro off the top, and rub.

- For 15 minutes, rub constantly on the limited area until it gets numb.

- Do this every night—even for a week after all the pain goes away.

- It is the direct contact of ice, and the constant massage rub that seems to do the job.

## Making your comeback after an injury

*It helps to have a good doctor*
When you are injured, a doctor can guide you during the crucial period as you return to running. You should get an OK from your doctor before taking your first run. During the comeback, when aches and pains arise and you have questions about when to move into speedwork or racing, an experienced doctor can help you avoid a re-injury.

### Do alternative exercise while sidelined

If the injury is not aggravated by alternative exercise, do it during your injury "time out." Clear any exercise with your doctor. The most beneficial for running is water running (see the section on cross training in this book). In fact, I know of many runners who have maintained most of their fitness by running in the water during an injury. The best program is to water-run about the same number of minutes per day you would do when running on land—at about the same feeling of exertion.

### Ease back into running—every other day, lots of walking

The first few days back running are crucial. If you push a little too hard, you can bring back the injury quickly. Run every other day, and do lots of walking on the first 3-6 sessions. Remember that your mission during the first two weeks back is simply to get the legs and feet moving gently again.

### Stay below the threshold of further irritation

Most running injuries will heal while you get back into running if you are conservative. You don't want to feel even an ache in an injured body part during the first 2 weeks of your comeback. If it starts to hurt at 1 mile of slow running, run just .7 of a mile or three laps.

The same rule applies when you return to speedwork—stay below the number of repetitions that aggravate the injured area. Another way of saying this is that you should stop the workout before you feel a possible return of the injury.

### Watch the speedwork

When you get the go-ahead to start speedwork again, be very conservative. In the first few workouts, run the first part of the first few repetitions very slowly. In each one, you should gradually pick up the pace. Just as your return to slow running, the first few speed sessions are designed to get your legs adapting to the faster running—don't worry about the pace.

For more info on coming back from injury, see *Galloway's Book on Running*.

# Preventing injury

I think of myself as a "prevention specialist." It is my mission to help you to avoid aches, pains, time off from running and visits to the doctor. So, as one runner to another, here are my top ways to stay injury free.

## Take 48 hours between runs

Speed training puts a lot more stress on the muscles than just running. Allowing the running muscles to rest the day before a workout will leave the muscles, joints, etc. resilient for the workout.

Taking the day off after a workout will allow for maximum recovery. Stair machine work should also be avoided during the 48 hour rest period (stair work uses the same muscles as running). Also avoid any other activities that irritate any area that aches, and could be prone to injury.

## Don't stretch!

A high percentage of the injured runners who I work with in our training programs and e-coaching have either become injured because they stretched, or aggravated the injury by stretching. When they stop stretching, a significant percentage report that the injury heals enough to run in a relatively short period of time. For more info on stretching, see the "Stretching" chapter. The exception to this rule is when you have Ilio-tibial band injury. For this injury alone, stretching the I-T band seems to help runners continue to run while they heal.

## Do the "toe squincher" exercise

This exercise can be done 10-30 times a day on both feet (one at a time). Point the toes and squinch them until the foot cramps (only a few seconds). This strengthens the many little muscles in the foot that can provide a platform of support. It is particularly effective in preventing plantar fascia. You can do this with your shoes on or off.

## Don't increase total mileage more than 10% a week

Monitor your mileage that you run in your journal or calendar. If you exceed the 10 per cent increase on a given week, take an extra day off the following week.

## Drop total mileage in half, every 3rd week

—even when increasing by no more than 10% per week. Your log book can help you monitor this. Cutting mileage every 3rd week won't cause you to lose any conditioning and you'll help the body heal itself. A steady increase, week after week, does not allow the legs to catch up and rebuild.

## Avoid a long stride—both walking and running

Running with more of a shuffle (feet close to the ground) reduces the chance of many injuries. Even walking with a long stride can irritate the shin muscles. The most common running injuries due to form are the result of an over-stride. Read the "Running Form" section for more information on developing an efficient running form.

## At the first sign of pain, take 1-3 days off

Don't keep running when there is pain, inflammation or loss of function in the potentially injured area. It is always better to take time off for healing.

# TROUBLE-SHOOTING ACHES AND PAINS

**A**t the first sign of soreness or irritation in these areas, read the injury chapter. It is always better to take 2-3 days off from running, go through appropriate treatment, and then start back making some form adjustments. In most of these areas, I've found that stretching aggravates the problem.

For more information, see *Galloway's Book on Running*.

## Shins:

I. **Soreness or pain in the front of the shin (anterior tibial area)**

# Note

Even after you make the corrections, shin problems often take several weeks to heal. As long as the shin problem is not a stress fracture, easy running can often allow it to heal as quickly (or more quickly) than complete layoff. In general, most runners can run when they have shin splints—they just need to stay below the threshold of further irritation.

## Causes:

1. Increasing too rapidly—either too many miles per week, or too much speedwork too soon
2. Running too fast, even on one day—most commonly, running faster on the speed repetitions
3. Running or walking with a stride that is too long—shorten stride and use more of a "shuffle"

II. **Soreness or pain at the inside of the lower leg (posterior tibial area)**

## Causes:

1. Same three causes as in anterior tibial shin splints above
2. More common with runners who over-pronate. This means that they tend to roll to the inside of the foot as they push off.
3. Shoes may be too soft, allowing a floppy/pronated foot to roll inward more than usual

**Corrections:**

1. Reduce stride length.
2. Put more walking into your run-walk ratio from the beginning.
3. If you are an over-pronator on the forward part of your feet, get a stable, motion control shoe.
4. Ask your foot doctor if there is a foot device that can help you.

# Shoulder and neck muscles: tired and tight

**Primary Cause:** leaning too far forward as you run

**Other Causes:**

1. Holding arms too far away from the body as you run
2. Swinging arms and shoulders too much as you run

**Corrections:**

1. Use the "puppet on a string" image (detailed in the "Running Form" chapter) about every 4-5 minutes during all runs and walks, particularly the longer ones. This is noted in the section on posture.
2. Watch how you are holding your arms. Try to keep the arms close to the body
3. Minimize the swing of your arms. Keep the hands close to the body, lightly touching your shirt or the outside of your shorts as your arms swing.

# Lower Back: tight, sore, or painful after a run

## Causes:
1. Leaning too far forward as you run
2. Having a stride length that is too long for you

## Corrections:
1. Use the "puppet on a string" image several times on all runs and walks, particularly the longer ones. This is noted in the next chapter on "Running Form," in the section on posture.
2. Ask a physical therapist whether some strengthening exercise can help.
3. When in doubt, shorten your stride length.

## Knees

### I. Pain at the end of a run

## Causes:
1. Stride length could be too long
2. Doing too much, too soon
3. Not inserting enough walk breaks regularly, from the beginning
4. When the main running muscles get tired, you will tend to wobble from side to side.

## Corrections:
1. Shorten the stride.
2. Stay closer to the ground, using more of a shuffle.
3. Monitor your mileage in a log book, and hold your increase to less than 10% a week.
4. Use more walk breaks during your run.
5. Start at a slower pace.

## II. On the side of the knee—sometimes other areas on the outside of the leg and hip

This is often Iliotibial Band Syndrome (stretches from hip to knee on outside of leg).

### Causes:
1. Stride length could be too long
2. Doing too much, too soon
3. Not inserting enough walk breaks regularly, from the beginning
4. Pushing 2 or 3 more repetitions or 1-2 miles—when you're exhausted and wobbling
5. When the main running muscles get tired, you will tend to wobble from side to side.

### Corrections:
1. Shorten the stride.
2. Stay closer to the ground, using more of a shuffle.
3. Monitor your mileage in a log book, and hold your increase to less than 10% a week.
4. Use more walk breaks during your run.
5. Start at a slower pace.
6. Stretch the Iliotibial band.
7. Don't run on a slant—run on the flat.
8. If you suspect that running the turns on the track produces this, measure a straight course for speed segments.

## III. Behind the knee: pain, tightness, or continued soreness or weakness

### Causes:
1. Stretching
2. Over striding—particularly at the end of long runs, speed sessions, or races

### Corrections:
1. Don't stretch.
2. Shorten the stride—especially at end of a run or the end of a workout.
3. Keep your feet low to the ground.

# Hamstrings: tightness, soreness, or pain

### Causes:
1. Stretching
2. Stride length too long
3. Lifting the foot too high behind as your leg swings back

### Corrections:
1. Don't stretch.
2. Maintain a short stride, keeping the hamstring relaxed—especially at the end of the run.
3. Take more walking early in the run, possibly throughout the run.
4. As the leg swings behind you, let the lower leg rise no higher than a position that is parallel to the horizontal before swinging forward again.
5. Deep tissue massage can sometimes help with this muscle group.

# Quadriceps (front of the thigh): sore, tired, painful

## Causes:
1. Lifting your leg and knee too high, especially when tired
2. Using the quads to slow down going downhill, because you were running too fast

## Corrections:
1. Maintain little or no knee lift, especially at the end of your run.
2. Run with a shuffle—keep your feet low to the ground.
3. Let your stride get very short at the top of hills, and when tired, don't lengthen it.
4. If you are running too fast going down hills, keep shortening the stride until you slow down, and/or take more walk breaks on the downhill.

# Sore feet or lower legs

## Causes:
1. Too much bounce
2. Pushing off too hard
3. Shoes don't fit correctly or are too worn out
4. Insole of shoe is worn out

## Corrections:
1. Keep your feet low to the ground.
2. Maintain a light touch of the feet.
3. Get a shoe check to see if your shoes are too worn.
4. You may need only a new insole.

# RUNNING FORM— TO RUN EASIER AND FASTER

*"You may be a few form improvements away from a faster time."*

**W**ould you like to run easier, faster, lighter on your feet, and have fewer aches and pains? By taking action now, and making a few minor adjustments, you can do this, and feel so much better as you run. You have an internal advocate: your right brain. You see, the repeated motion of running thousands of steps—especially when running fast— stimulates your right brain to eliminate inefficient motion as it programs your body to run the easiest way. The regularity of speed workouts stimulates further efficiency in your range of motion.

After having analyzed over 10,000 runners in my running schools and weekend retreats, I've found that most runners are running very close to their ideal efficiency. The mistakes are seldom big ones. But a series of small mistakes can slow you down or create major aches, pains, and sometimes injuries. By making a few minor adjustments, most runners can feel better and run faster.

Faster runners tend to make mistakes that cost them seconds and sometimes minutes in races. Before I detail these common problems, let's look at some principles of running for distances longer than 200 meters (half a lap around a track).

## I believe that running is an inertia activity

This means that your primary mission is to maintain your momentum. Very little strength is needed to run—even to run fast for 800 meters and up. The first hundred meters should get your body into the motion and rhythm for your run. After that, the best strategy is to conserve energy while maintaining that forward inertia. To reduce fatigue, aches and pains, your right brain, helped by muscle memory, intuitively fine-tunes your mechanics and motion to minimize effort.

Humans have many bio-mechanical adaptations working for them, which have been made more efficient over more than a million years of walking and running. The anatomical origin of efficiency in humans begins with the ankle and Achilles tendon, which I will treat as one extremely sophisticated system of levers, springs, balancing devices, and more. Biomechanics experts believe that this degree of development was not needed for walking. When our ancient ancestors had to run to survive, the evolution reached a new level of performance.

Through a series of speed sessions and drills, you can maximize use of the Achilles and ankle, so that a very little amount of muscle work produces a quicker, consistent forward movement. During the first few speed sessions your legs may be a little sore. But as you get in better and better shape, with improved endurance, you'll find yourself going farther and faster with little or no increased effort. Other muscle groups offer support and help to fine-tune the process. When you feel aches and pains that might be due to the way you run, going back to the minimal use of the ankle and Achilles tendon can often leave you feeling smooth and efficient very quickly.

## Three negative results of inefficient form:

1. Fatigue from extraneous motions becomes so severe that it takes much longer to recover.
2. Muscles or tendons are pushed so far beyond their limits that they break down and become injured—or just hurt.
3. The experience is so negative that the desire to run is reduced, producing burnout.

It all starts with general fatigue that stresses your weak links. For example, if your knee gets weakened at the end of a workout or a race, and you keep pushing to maintain pace, your body will use other muscles and tendons to keep you going. You start to "wobble," as these alternatives are not designed to do the job. Continued pushing will aggravate these other tendons, etc.

There is also a counter-productive tendency to extend stride length at the end of a tiring run. This may keep you at the same pace for a while—at the expense of the quads, hamstrings, and several other components that are over-stressed. It is always the safer option to cut stride, and get back into a smooth motion when you feel even a slight aggravation at the end of a run. It's OK to push through tiredness when running smoothly, as long as you are not feeling pain in any area. But if this means extending stride or wobbling (which aggravates your weak links), it's not OK.

I don't suggest that everyone should try to create perfect form. But when you become aware of your form problems, and make changes to keep them from producing aches and pains, you'll run smoother, reduce fatigue, and run faster.

## Your own form check

In some of my clinics, I use a digital camera that gives instant feedback. If you have one of these cameras, have a friend take pictures of you running, from the side (not running towards or away from the camera) while you run on a flat surface. Some runners can check themselves while running alongside stores that offer a reflection in a plate glass window. Here's what to look for.

## Relaxed muscles at the end of the run

Overall, the running motion should feel smooth, and there should be no tension in your neck, back, shoulders or legs. Even during the last half mile of a hard workout or race, try to maintain the three main elements of good form, and you'll stay relaxed. You should not try to push through tightness and pain. Adjust your form to reduce these adversities.

## The big three: posture, stride, and bounce

In thousands of individual running form consultations, I've discovered that when runners have problems, they tend to occur in these three areas. Often the problems are like a signature, tending to be very specific to the areas that you overuse, because of your unique movement patterns. By making a few small changes in your running form, you can reduce or eliminate the problems.

# I. Posture

Good running posture is actually good body posture. The head is naturally balanced over the shoulders, which are aligned over the hips. As the foot comes underneath, all of these elements are in balance, so that no energy is needed to prop up the body. You shouldn't have to work to pull a wayward body back from a wobble or inefficient motion.

### *Forward lean—the most common mistake*
The posture errors tend to be mostly due to a forward lean, especially when we are tired. The head wants to get to the finish as soon as possible, but the legs can't go any faster. A common tendency at the end of a speed session is to lean with the head. In races, this results in more than a few falls around the finish line. A forward lean will often concentrate fatigue, soreness, and tightness in the lower back, or neck. Biomechanics experts note that a forward lean will reduce stride length, causing a slowdown or an increase in effort.

It all starts with the head. When the neck muscles are relaxed, the head is more free to find an alignment that is naturally balanced on the shoulders. If there is tension in the neck, or soreness afterward, the head is usually leaning too far forward. This triggers a more general upper body imbalance, in which the head and chest are suspended slightly ahead of the hips and feet. Ask a running companion to tell you if and when your head is too far forward, or leaning down. This usually occurs at the end of a tiring run.

The ideal position of the head is mostly upright, with your eyes focused about 30-40 yards ahead of you.

### Sitting back

The hips are the other major postural component that can easily get out of alignment. A runner with this problem, when observed from the side, will have the butt behind the rest of the body. When the pelvis area is shifted back, the legs are not allowed to go through a natural range of motion, and the stride length becomes shorter than ideal. This produces a slower pace, even when spending significant effort. Many runners tend to hit harder on their heels when their hips are shifted back.

### A backward lean is rare

It is rare for runners to lean back, but it happens. In my experience, this is usually due to a structural problem in the spine or hips. If you do this, and you're having pain in the neck, back or hips, you should see a doctor. One symptom is excessive shoe wear on the back of the heel, but there are other reasons why you may show this kind of wear.

### Correction: "Puppet on a string"

The best correction I've found to postural problems has been this mental exercise: imagine that you are a puppet on a string. Suspended from up above like a puppet—from the head and each side of the shoulders. In this way, your head lines up above the shoulders, the hips come directly underneath, and the feet naturally touch lightly directly underneath. It won't hurt anyone to do the "puppet" several times during a run.

It helps to combine this image with a deep breath. About every 4-5 minutes, as you start to run after a walk break, take a deep, lower lung breath, straighten up and say "I'm a puppet." Then imagine that you don't have to spend energy maintaining this upright posture, because the strings attached from above keep you on track. As you continue to do this, you reinforce good posture, and the behavior can become a good habit.

Upright posture not only allows you to stay relaxed, you will probably improve stride length. When you lean forward, you'll be cutting your stride to stay balanced. When you straighten up, you'll receive a stride bonus of an inch or so, without any increase in energy. Note: don't try to increase stride length. When it happens naturally, you won't feel it—you'll just run faster.

### An oxygen dividend
Breathing improves when you straighten up. A leaning body can't get ideal use out of the lower lungs. This can cause side pain. When you run upright, the lower lungs can receive adequate air, maximize oxygen absorption, and reduce the chance of side pain.

## II. Feet low to the ground
The most efficient stride is a shuffle with feet right next to the ground. As long as you pick your foot up enough to avoid stumbling over a rock or uneven pavement, stay low to the ground. Most runners don't need to get more than 1" clearance—even when running fast. As you increase speed and ankle action, you will come off the ground a bit more than this. Again, don't try to increase stride, let this happen naturally.

Your ankle combined with your Achilles tendon will act as a spring, moving you forward on each running step. If you stay low to the ground, very little effort is required. Through this "shuffling" technique, running becomes almost automatic. When runners err on bounce, they try to push off too hard. This usually results in extra effort spent in lifting the body off the ground. You can think of this as energy wasted in the air—energy that could be used to run faster.

The other negative force that penalizes a higher bounce is that of gravity. The higher you rise, the harder you fall. Each additional bounce off the ground delivers a lot more impact on feet and legs, which during speed sessions, races, and long runs, produces aches, pains and injuries.

### The correction for too much bounce: light touch
The ideal foot "touch" should be so light that you don't usually feel yourself pushing off or landing. This means that your foot stays low to the ground and goes through an efficient and natural motion. Instead of trying to overcome gravity, you get in synch with it. If your foot "slaps" when you run, you will definitely improve with a lighter touch.

Here's a "light touch drill":   During the middle of a run, time yourself for 20 seconds. Focus on one item: touching so softly that you don't hear your feet. Earplugs are not allowed for this drill. Imagine that you are running on thin ice or through a bed of hot coals. Do several of these 20 second touches, becoming quieter and quieter. You should feel very little impact on your feet as you do this drill.

## III. Stride length
Studies have shown that as runners get faster, the stride length shortens. This clearly shows that the key to faster and more efficient running is increased cadence or quicker

turnover of feet and legs. A major cause of aches, pains and injuries is a stride length that is too long. When in doubt, it is always better to err on the side of having a shorter stride.

### Don't lift your knees!

Even most of the world class distance runners don't have a high knee lift. When your knees go too high, you are over-using the quadriceps muscle (front of the thigh), resulting in a stride that is too long to be efficient. The most common time when runners stride too long is at the end of a tiring run. This slight overstride when the legs are tired will leave your quads sore the next day or two.

### Don't kick out too far in front of you!

If you watch the natural movement of the leg, it will kick forward slightly as the foot gently moves forward in the running motion to contact the ground. Let this be a natural motion that produces no tightness in the muscles behind the lower or upper leg.

Tightness in the front of the shin, or behind the knee, or in the hamstring (back of the thigh) is a sign that you are kicking too far forward, and reaching out too far. Correct this by staying low to the ground, shortening the stride, and lightly touching the ground.

SHOES

*"The best advice about running shoes…*
*is to get the best advice."*

Shoes are the only equipment that you need for running, but they can make a big difference in how you feel when you run. Some can even help you run faster. While it is unlikely that you will get injured with the wrong pair, you may not get into a comfortable rhythm if your feet are not matched to the right shoe. Slight changes in the way the foot lands can produce more aches, pains and longer recovery time. A smooth and fast rhythm starts with the foot and can mean faster race times.

Each shoe made for running is designed for a particular type of foot and how that foot operates. You have a better chance today of getting a shoe that enhances the way you run. But a good shoe store can help you sort through the confusion of models, devices, and hype. Without the right guidance, it's easier to get a shoe that was designed for someone else's foot.

# Fitting tips:

## Get the best advice

It would be ideal to find a store that specializes in running. With staff members who understand how the foot works when you run, and are trained in matching feet with the right shoes, you're more likely to find shoes that work for you. If you don't have a store like this in your area, follow the directions at the end of this chapter.

## Bring with you a worn out pair of shoes—walking or running

A well-worn shoe reveals the way your foot rolls, which is the best indicator of how your foot functions. A street shoe that shows great wear on the bottom is often the best guide for a shoe expert. Running shoes often don't show a lot of wear on the bottom because the midsole gives out before the outer sole shows a pattern of foot movement.

## A store staff person can also note the way your foot functions

Since shoes are made in categories, and each category is designed to support and enhance a type of foot, you want to get one designed for your foot. By watching you walk and run, a trained eye can note how your foot rolls, and recommend a few shoes.

## Give and take

Tell the staff person which shoes worked for you in the past, and which did not. As you try each shoe, explain whether you feel better running in one versus the others. Point out any pressure areas or problems in fit.

## Buy the training shoe first

At first, you'll need a pair for long runs and easy running days. If you need a lot of motion control devices (explained below) to protect you from injury, this shoe may slow you down in races by being too heavy and "clunky." In your first visit to the shoe store, at least look at the racing shoes and the light weight training shoes. Wait until you are several weeks into your training before you decide to get a racing shoe.

## Do I need a racing shoe?

In most cases, racing shoes only speed you up a few seconds a mile. If this amount of time will make a difference, go through the fitting process a second time. Be sure to bring in your training shoes, and tell the staff person whether you have a motion control training shoe. If you get a racing shoe, break it in gradually to avoid blisters.

## Note any injuries or foot problems

You'll also want to tell the staff person about any past running injuries—or structural problems you have that affect your running. If you have had problems due to over-pronation, (see "floppy foot" below) you may need to get a shoe that can limit this from happening. An experienced staff person can advise.

## Don't try to fix your foot if it isn't broken

Even if your foot rolls excessively one way or the other, you don't necessarily need to get an over-controlling shoe. The leg and foot make many adjustments and adaptations which keep many runners injury free, even when they have extreme motion.

## The most expensive shoe is not the fastest or best shoe for most runners

Don't think that a high price will buy you a faster time or extra protection. Most runners find that the medium price shoes work best. Again, get the shoe that works best on your foot.

## How racing shoes can improve your time

Because of the weight reduction alone, racing shoes can speed you up several seconds in a 2 mile. But this can be a double-edged sword. The light material used in racing shoes will compress more quickly. Heavier runners will not only break these down, they may also find that the cushion is significantly reduced at the end of their race. This is more of an issue in 5K and longer races, but ask your shoe expert about this.

Racing shoes are also designed to allow the foot to move through the running motion more quickly. This means that they don't have the motion control devices of stable training shoes. Only a few runners have motion control problems that are severe enough to prohibit them from using a racing shoe. But ask your shoe expert if the increased freedom of motion of the "quick" shoes may allow for extraneous motions that are not the best for your foot or leg.

The fit of a racing shoe is usually tighter than that of a training shoe. As you fit a racing shoe, lace them up very snugly. Run outside on the pavement, doing a few accelerations. You need to know how the shoe feels as you run fast in the shoe.

Psychologically, racing shoes will give you an edge. As you lace up the shoes you mentally shift into the mindset to race. When you put on the right racing shoe, you feel lighter and quicker, which gives you a mental edge when you run. As noted in the "Mental Toughness" chapter of this book, mindset can mean the difference between breaking your record or not.

**Overall:** The best advice about shoes can come from the staff of a really good technical running store.

## If you don't have a running store in your area...

1.  Look at the wear pattern on your most worn pair of walking or running shoes. Use the guide below to help you choose about 3 pairs of shoes from one of the categories below:

✔ **Floppy?**
If you have the wear pattern of a "floppy" or flexible foot on the inside of the forefoot, and have some foot or knee pain, look at a shoe that has "structure" or anti-pronation capabilities.

✔ **Rigid?**
If you have a wear pattern on the outside of the forefoot of the shoe, and no wear on the inside, you probably have a rigid foot, and can choose a neutral shoe that has adequate cushion and flexibility for you, as you run and walk in them.

? **Can't tell?**
Choose shoes that are neutral or have mid range of cushion and support.

1. Set aside at least 30 minutes to choose your next shoe.

2. Run and walk on a pavement surface to compare the shoes. If you have a floppy foot, make sure that you get the support you need.

3. You want a shoe that feels natural on your foot—no pressure or aggravation—while allowing the foot to go through the range of motion needed for running.

4. Again, take as much time as you need before deciding.

5. If the store doesn't let you run in the shoe, go to another store.

## Go by fit and not the size noted on the box of the shoe

Most runners wear a running shoe that is about 2 sizes larger than their street shoe. For example, I wear a size 10 street shoe, but run in a size 12 running model. Be open to getting the best fit, regardless of what size you see on the running shoe box.

## Extra room for your toes

Your foot tends to swell during the day, so it's best to fit your shoes after noontime. Be sure to stand up in the shoe during the fitting process to measure how much extra room you have in the toe region of the shoe. Pay attention to the longest part of your feet, and leave at least half an inch.

## Width issues

- Running shoes tend to be a bit wider than street shoes.
- Usually, the lacing can "snug up" the difference if your foot is a bit narrower.
- The shoe shouldn't be laced too tight around your foot because the foot swells during running and walking. On hot days, the average runner will move up one-half shoe size.
- In general, running shoes are designed to handle a certain amount of "looseness." But if you are getting blisters when wearing a loose shoe, tighten the laces.
- Several shoe companies have some shoes in widths.
- The shoe is too narrow if you are rolling off the edge of the shoe as you push off—on either side.

## Shoes for women

Women's shoes tend to be slightly narrower than those for men, and the heel is usually a bit smaller. The quality of the major running shoe brands is equal, whether for men or women. But, about 25% of women runners have feet that can fit better into men's shoes. Usually the confusion comes when women wear large sizes. The better running stores can help you make a choice in this area.

## Breaking in a new shoe

- Wear the new shoe around the house, for an hour or more each day for a week. If you stay on carpet, and the shoe doesn't fit correctly, you can exchange it at the store. But, if you have put some wear on the shoe, dirt, etc., few stores will take it back.
- In most cases you will find that the shoe feels comfortable enough to run immediately. It is best to

continue walking in the shoe, gradually allowing the foot to accommodate to the arch, the heel, the ankle pads, and to make other adjustments. If you run in the shoe too soon, blisters are often the result.

- If there are no rubbing issues on the foot when walking, you could walk in the new shoe for a gradually increasing amount. For 2-4 days.

- On the first run, just run about half a mile in the shoe. Put on your old shoes and continue the run.

- On each successive run, increase the distance run in the new shoe for 3-4 runs. At this point, you will usually have the new shoe broken in.

## How do you know when it's time to get a new shoe?

1. When you have been using a shoe for 3-4 weeks successfully, buy another pair of exactly the same model, make, size, etc. The reason for this is that the shoe companies often make significant changes or discontinue shoe models (even successful ones) every 6-8 months.

2. Walk around the house in the new shoe for a few days.

3. After the shoe feels broken in, run the first half mile of one of your weekly runs in the new shoe, then put on the shoe that is already broken in.

4. On the "shoe break-in" day, gradually run a little more in the new shoe. Continue to do this only one day a week.

5. Several weeks later you will notice that the new shoe offers more bounce than the old one.

6. When the old shoe doesn't offer the support you need, shift to the new pair.

7. Start breaking in a third pair.

# DRESSING FOR SUCCESS

After years of working with people in various climates, here are my recommendations for the appropriate clothing, based upon the temperature. First, choose garments that will be comfortable, especially next to your skin, and especially at the end of a run. You may have to resist the temptation to buy a fashion color, but function is most important. Watch for seams and bunching up in areas where you will have body parts rubbing together thousands of times during a run.

Cotton is usually not a good fabric for those who perspire a great deal. The cotton will absorb the sweat, hold it next to your skin, and increase the weight you must carry during the run. Garments made out of fabric labeled Polypro, Coolmax, Drifit, etc., hold enough body heat close to you in winter, while releasing extra heat. In summer and winter, they move moisture away from the skin, cooling you in hot weather, and avoiding a chill in the winter, and limiting the weight increase from perspiration.

| Temperature | What to wear |
|---|---|
| 14°C or 60°F and above | Tank top or singlet, and shorts |
| 9 to13°C or 50 to 59°F | T-shirt and shorts |
| 5 to 8°C or 40 to 49°F | Long sleeve light weight shirt, shorts or tights (or nylon long pants) mittens and gloves |
| 0 to 4°C or 30 to 39°F | Long sleeve medium weight shirt, and another T-shirt, tights and shorts, socks or mittens or gloves, and a hat over the ears |
| -4 to -1°C or 20-29°F | Medium weight long sleeve shirt, another T-shirt, tights and shorts, socks, mittens or gloves, and a hat over the ears |
| -8 to -3°C or 10-19°F | Medium weight long sleeve shirt, and medium/heavy weight shirt, tights and shorts, nylon wind suit, top and pants, socks, thick mittens, and a hat over the ears |
| -12 to -7°C or 0-9°F | Two medium or heavyweight long sleeve tops, thick tights, thick underwear (especially for men), Medium to heavy warm up, gloves and thick mittens, ski mask, a hat over the ears, and vaseline covering any exposed skin. |

| Temperature | What to wear |
|---|---|
| -18 to -11°C or -15°F | Two heavyweight long sleeve tops, tights and thick tights, thick underwear (and supporter for men), thick warm up (top and pants) mittens over gloves, thick ski mask, and a hat over ears, vasoline covering any exposed skin, thicker socks on your feet and other foot protection, as needed. |
| Minus 20° both C & F | Add layers as needed |

## What not to wear

1. *A heavy coat in winter.* If the layer is too thick, you'll heat up, sweat excessively, and cool too much when you take it off.

2. *No shirt for men in summer.* Fabric that holds some of the moisture will give you more of a cooling effect as you run and walk.

3. *Too much sun screen*—it can interfere with sweating.

4. *Socks that are too thick in summer.* Your feet swell and the pressure from the socks can increase the chance of a black toenail and blisters.

5. *Lime green shirt with bright pink polka dots* (unless you have a lot of confidence and/or can run fast).

## Special cases

Chaffing can be reduced by lycra and other fabric. Many runners have eliminated chaffing between the legs by using a lycra "bike tight" as an undergarment. These are also called "lycra shorts." There are several skin lubricants on the market, including Glide.

Some men suffer from irritation of their nipples. Having a slick and smooth fabric across the chest will reduce this. There is now a product called Nip-Guard that has allowed many men to completely avoid the problem.

# STRETCHING

*"Stretching causes many injuries."*

It may surprise you to learn this, but I'm not a big advocate of stretching. After having worked with tens of thousands of runners, and conducting surveys, I've discovered that those who stretch regularly have more injuries—often as a direct result of stretching. While there are some specific stretches that help some individuals, I believe that most people who run and walk don't need to stretch at all.

In many other sports, like tennis, basketball, soccer, golf, etc., stretching warms the muscles up, for activities that the body was not designed to do. Running is significantly different than those other activities. We were designed to run and walk long distances—our ancient ancestors covered thousands of miles a year! Stretching pushes the tendons and muscles beyond what they are currently ready to do, often into injury.

## In general, don't try to stretch out tightness

As you run regularly, and do some speedwork, you will get tighter. Don't be alarmed, because most of this comes from muscle fatigue, and the waste products that are deposited as you continue to run. Stretching will not take away this type of tightness.

*A false sense of relief.* I fully admit that if you stretch a tired, tight muscle, it feels better...for a short period. After talking to dozens of physiologists, orthopedists, and other specialists, I've come to understand that stretching a tight muscle results in many small tears of the muscle fibers. Your body senses this and sends hormones to kill the pain. Even one stretch under these conditions can injure a muscle, and definitely increases recovery time as your body repairs the stretching damage. Even with light stretching, you will tend to weaken the muscle.

*Some tightness is good.* Your body will get a bit tighter as you run, for a while. This is due to the legs adapting to distance running. Your push from the foot is more effective and your range of motion more efficient. I've been told by many biomechanics experts that this type of tightness in most cases reduces the chance of injury and makes running easier.

*Stretching before a race or speed workout often produces injury.* Don't stretch because you see other runners go through their own rituals. The best way to warm up a tight muscle is to walk for 5 minutes, do a very gentle walk-run for 10 minutes, do 4-8 acceleration gliders, and then walk for 5 minutes.

*Massage can work out tightness.* If you are having a problem with tightness in a certain part of the body, massage can help—even using the self help massage tools, such as "the stick."

## Yoga and Pilates?

I communicate with runners about every week who get injured because they stretched too far during these programs. Even mild stretches that are outside your range of motion can be adverse to the joints and tendons. For some yoga practitioners, however, the philosophical benefits of yoga can be as significant as those from running. Many competitors use yoga to help them relax. If you enjoy such mental benefits go through the sessions, but don't stretch.

## Ilio-tibial band injury—the only major exception

The ilio-tibial is a band of fascia that acts as a tendon. It starts at the hip and continues along the outside of each leg, attaching in several places below the knee. Besides the stretch noted here, individuals find that there are specific stretches that will help to release the tightness of their I-T band. Those who suffer from this injury can stretch before, after, or during a run, or whenever it tightens up and/or starts to hurt. There is more on this injury in the injury-free section of this book.

## Don't feel guilty if you don't stretch before you run-walk

A gentle walk for 5 minutes, followed by a very gradual transition from walking to run-walk has been the most effective warm up that I have found.

## If you have individual stretches that work.... DO THEM!

I've met several people who have certain stretches that seem to help them. If you find a stretch that works for you, go ahead. Just be careful.

# STRENGTHENING

There are a few strengthening exercises that I feel will help your running. But overall, I don't believe that running is a strength activity. As noted in the "Running Form" chapter, running is done most effectively, in my opinion, when you use your momentum—your inertia. The strength you need for running is minimal.

For proof, just look at the physiques of the faster distance and middle distance runners. There is hardly any muscle development, and no bulk. Carrying around extra superstructure (and weight) that doesn't help you move forward is extra work for the body, causing a slowdown later in a long run. In strength contests with other athletes that I have attended, distance runners tend to score at the bottom. When I competed at the world-class level, I didn't know a single competitor who spent an hour doing weight work on a regular basis, unless their high school or college track coach made them do it.

# Note

These exercises are not meant to be prescriptions for medical problems. They are offered from one runner to another, because runners have reported benefit from them. If you have a back or other medical issue, make sure your doctor and other specialists give you an OK to use these or any exercises.

## Strength for the postural muscles

By balancing the strength of muscles that support your posture and keep you upright, you'll tend to maintain the posture that you have—or improve it. When you run upright, running is easier, and you can run a little faster. You'll move forward more efficiently with less energy required for keeping your body balanced—and you won't get as tired.

Good postural muscles will also help you to breathe more efficiently. When upright, you can breathe deeply, maximizing oxygen absorption and reducing or eliminating side pains, most commonly called "side cramps."

There are two groups of muscles that need to be strengthened. On the front side, the abdominal group provides support and balance. When "ab" strength is balanced by back and shoulder muscles, you will resist fatigue in the shoulders, neck, and back.

## Front muscles: the crunch

Lie on your back on a cushioned carpet or floor pad with adequate cushioning for your back. Bend your knees. Now raise your head and upper back very slightly off the floor.

Go up an inch or two, and down again, but don't let the upper back hit the floor. As you move very slightly, don't let the stomach muscles relax—keep them working as you go up and down in this very narrow range of motion. It also helps, as you are doing this, to roll slightly to either side, continuously moving. This strengthens the whole range of muscle groups that support the front side of your torso.

## For the back, shoulders and neck: arm running

Holding a dumbell (milk or water jug, or other weight) in each hand while standing (not while running) go through a range of motion that you would use when running. Keep the weights close to your body as the hands (with weights) swing from your waist up to your shoulders, and return.

Pick a weight that makes you feel, after a set of 10 repetitions, that you worked the muscles involved. But, don't have so much weight that you have to struggle as you do your last 1-2 reps. Start with one set of 10, and increase to 3-5 sets, once or twice a week. This can be done on a running day, or on a rest day.

## Prescriptive exercises

These are designed for those who feel that they need more support in one or more of the areas listed below. Those who have had regular aches, pains, or injuries in one of the areas below have received benefit from these exercises.

*Toe Squincher*—for prevention of injuries of the foot and lower leg

I believe that this exercise will help every person that runs and walks, but is particularly helpful for those doing speedwork. Whether barefooted or not, point your toes and contract the muscles of your foot until they cramp. It only takes a few seconds for this to happen. You can repeat this exercise 10-30 times a day, every day. This is the best way I know to prevent a foot injury called plantar fascia, but it strengthens the areas all over the foot and ankle for better support. I've also heard from runners who believe it has helped to prevent Achilles tendon problems.

## Knees—the stiff leg lift

If you have knee problems, here is an exercise that strengthens the various muscles in the thigh, the quadriceps, or "quads." By developing strength in the range of muscles above, you can tighten the connections around the knee, providing better support. When the muscle group that is strengthened, the quads, gains strength, you can do a better job of keeping your foot in a small range of motion directly below the hips. With this mechanical set-up, the knee has less stress.

Sit on a tall bench or table. Keeping the knee straight out, lift the leg up and down, gradually changing the range of motion from inside to outside. Start with no weight, and one set of 10 lifts. When you can easily do 3 sets of 10 lifts with each leg, add a few pounds using a bag or pocketbook, looped around the ankle.

## Note

Do this exercise after a run on a running day.

## Shins—2 exercises

### The foot lift

Sit on a bench with the knee bent at a right angle. Your foot must be significantly off the floor. Hang a bag or pocket book with a pound of weight over the foot. Lift your foot up and down 10 times. Move the angle of the foot to the inside and the outside. Add more weight as a set of 10 feels easy.

### Heel walking

Use a very padded shoe. Walk on your heels, so that your toe region is off the floor. Start with 10 steps, and increase until you can do 2-3 sets of 20-30 steps.

## Note

Do this exercise after a run on a running day.

# RACE DAY

**A**fter having run in races every year since 1958, I've come to believe that success comes from getting the "little things" right. As you prepare for the big day, you will be organizing yourself, gaining mental focus, reducing tension, anticipating problems as you gear up to solve them. All of this sets yourself up for success.

In this chapter I will try to cover the most crucial areas that you will need to prepare for on race day. But you will need to customize this based upon your needs, race venue, lifestyle, etc. Keep fine-tuning your procedures as you go through the lists over and over again. You should get more confident with each trip.

# Rehearsal

Use your speed workouts as "dress rehearsals" for your big day. Since you may be nervous, bring your checklists, and go through everything as you will do at the race itself. If at all possible, run on the race course several times. If you are running on a track in your "big test," work out on that track, if possible. You want to be familiar with every aspect of the environment surrounding the venue. Success may depend upon a feeling of confidence—that you own the venue. The more times you've been successful in workouts and runs at the track or race course, the more likely you'll feel this way.

If this is an important race that is out of town, it helps to visit there, run the course, and even stage a successful workout there. You'll learn the routes to use, where to park (or which rapid transit station to exit), and what the site is like. If you will be driving, drive into the parking area several times to make sure you understand how to go exactly where you need to park. This will help you to feel at home with the staging area on race day—reducing raceday anxiety. If it's a road course, run over the last half mile of the course at least twice—the most important part of the course to know. It's also beneficial to do the first mile of the course to see which side of the road is best for walk breaks (location of sidewalks, etc.). If your big race is on a track, visualize how you will be taking walk breaks, if you use them in the race.

Visualize your line up position. In a roadrace, you will be lining up in the area that corresponds with your pace. If you try to get ahead by lining up too far forward, you could slow down runners that are faster. In a roadrace, you want to visualize getting to the side of the road before taking walk breaks. On a track, you will be taking walk breaks to the outside.

## What to look for in choosing a roadrace

- Is the course flat enough and otherwise "fast enough?"

- Well organized: no long lines, easy to register, start goes off on time, water on the course, refreshments for all, even the slowest; no major problems

- Refreshments—some races have water, others have a buffet.

- A good T-shirt or other reward—you'll wear it with pride.

- The organizers focus on average or beginning runners.

### The afternoon before

Don't run the day before the race. You won't lose any conditioning if you take two days off from running leading up to the race. This is a personal issue and the number of days you do not run before a race is your choice.

Some races require you to pick up your race number, and sometimes your computer chip (explained below) the day before. Look at the website or the entry form for instructions about this. Most races allow you to pick up your materials on race day—but be sure.

## Race number

This is sometimes called a "bib number." It should be pinned on the front of the garment you'll be wearing when you cross the finish line. Ask your race organizing committee if you will have to wear a bib. If so, make sure you have 2-4 safety pins.

## Computer chip

More and more races are using technology that automatically records your race number and time as you cross the finish. You must wear a computer chip that is usually laced on the shoes, near the top. Some race result technology companies have a velcro band that is attached to the ankle or arm. Read the instructions to make sure you are attaching this correctly. Be sure to turn this in after the race. The officials have volunteers to collect them, so stop and take them off your shoe, etc. There is a steep fine ($) for those who don't turn in the chip.

## The carbo loading dinner

Some races have a dinner or pasta party the night before. At the dinner, you will usually chat with runners at your table, and enjoy the evening. Don't eat much, however. Many runners assume, mistakenly, that they must eat a lot of food the night before. This is actually counter-productive. It takes at least 24 hours for most of the food you eat to be processed and useable in a race, usually longer. There is nothing you can eat the evening before a race that will help you.

But eating too much, or foods that don't work for you, can be a real problem. A lot of food in your gut when you are bouncing up and down in a race is stressful. A very common and embarrassing situation occurs when the gut is emptied to relieve this stress. While you don't want to starve yourself the afternoon and evening before, the best strategy is to eat small meals or snacks that you know are easy for the body to digest, and taper down the amount as you get closer to bed time. As always, it's best to have done a "rehearsal" of eating, so that you know what works, how much, when to stop eating, and what foods to avoid. The evening before your morning runs is a good time to work on your eating plan so that you can replicate the successful routine leading up to race day.

## Drinking

The day before, drink when you are thirsty. If you haven't had a drink of water or sports drink in a couple of hours, drink half a cup to a cup (4-8 oz.) each hour. Don't drink a lot of fluid during the morning of the race itself. This can lead to bathroom breaks before the race or the desire to do so during the race itself. Many races have porto-johns around the course, but some do not. This is another reason to preview the venue, and note the locations of bathrooms. It is a very common practice for runners that have consumed too much fluid that morning to find a tree or alley along the course. The best solution for most runners is to drink 6-10 oz. of fluid about 2 hours before the race. Usually this is totally out of the system before the start.

## Drinking tip:

If you practice drinking before your long runs, you can find the right amount of fluid that works best for you on race day. Stage your drinks, so that you know when you will be taking potty breaks, comfortably before the start of the race itself.

## The night before

Eating is optional after 5pm. If you are hungry, have a light snack (or two) that you have tested before, and has not caused problems. Less is better, but don't go to bed hungry. Continue to have about 8 oz. of a good electrolyte beverage like Accelerade over the 2 hours before you go to bed.

Alcohol is not recommended the night before, because the effects of this central nervous system depressant carry over to the next morning. Some runners have no trouble having one glass of wine or beer, while others are better off with none. If you decide to have a drink, I suggest that you make it one portion.

Pack your bag and lay out your clothes, so that you don't have to think very much on race morning.

- Your watch, set up for the run-walk ratio you are using
- A pace chart, or wrist band, with lap times, or mile times
- Shoes
- Socks
- Shorts
- Top—see clothing thermometer
- Pin race number on the front of the garment in which you will be finishing
- A few extra safety pins for your race number, or bib number
- Water, Accelerade, pre-race and post race beverages (such as Endurox R4), and a cooler if you wish
- Food for the drive in, and the drive home
- Bandages, skin lubricant, any other first aid items you may need
- Cash for registration if you are doing race day registration (check for exact amount, including late fee)
- $ 25-40 for gas, food, parking, etc.
- Race chip, attached according to the race instructions

- A few jokes or stories to provide laughs or entertainment before the start
- A copy of the "race day checklist," which is just below this section

## Sleep

You may sleep well, or you may not. Don't worry about it if you don't sleep at all. Many runners I work with every year don't sleep at all the night before, and have the best race of their lives. Of course, don't try to go sleepless....but if it happens, it is not a problem.

## Race day checklist

*Photocopy* this list so that you will not only have a plan, but you can carry it out in a methodical way. Pack the list in your race bag. Don't try anything new the day of your race, except for health or safety issues. The only item which has been successfully used for the first time in a race is walk breaks. Even first time users benefit significantly. Otherwise, stick with your plan.

*Fluid and potty stops*—after you wake up, drink 4-6 oz. of water every half hour. If you have used a sports drink like Accelerade about 30 minutes before your runs, prepare it. Use a cooler if you wish. In order to avoid the bathroom stops, stop your fluid intake according to the timetable of what has worked for you before.

*Eat*—what you have eaten before your harder runs. It is OK not to eat at all before a race of 10K or less, unless you are a diabetic; then go with the plan that you and your doctor have worked out.

*Get your bearings*—walk around the site to find where you want to line up, and how you will get to the start. Choose a side of the road that has more shoulder or sidewalk for ease in taking walk breaks. If you are on a track, find a place where you can wait to line up, that makes you feel comfortable—this is your pre-race home.

*Register or pick up your race number*—if you already have all of your materials, you can bypass this step. If not, look at the signage in the registration area and get in the right line. Usually there is one for "race day registration," and one for those who registered online or in the mail, and need to pick up their numbers.

*Start your warm-up 40-50 min before the start.* If possible, go backwards on the course for about .5-.6 mi and turn around. If it is a track race, run on the track if possible, and imagine yourself approaching the finish line with strength after each lap. This will give you a preview of the most important part of your race—the finish. Here is the warm-up routine:

- Walk for 5 minutes, slowly.
- Walk at a normal walking pace for 3-5 minutes, with a relaxed and short stride.
- Start your watch for the ratio of running and walking that you are using and do this, running and walking, for 10 minutes.
- Walk around for 5-10 minutes.
- Do 4-8 acceleration-gliders that gradually get you up to the speed you will be running in the race.
- If you have time, walk around the staging area, read your jokes, laugh, relax.

- Get in position and pick one side of the road where you want to line up. If on a track, go to "your area" to wait for the start.
- When the road is closed, and runners are called onto the road, go to the curb and stay at the side of the road, near your preferred place. At the track, waiting for the start, visualize how you are going to start the race—comfortable and a bit conservative.

## After the start

Remember that you can control how you feel during and afterward by conservative pacing and walks.

- Stick with your race plan and the run/walk ratio that has worked for you—take every walk break, especially the first one.
- Be conservative in pacing for the first one-third of the race, and don't let yourself be pulled out too fast on the running portions.
- Stay with your plan. As people pass you who are running faster than you are planning, or are not taking walk breaks, tell yourself that you will catch them later—you will.
- If anyone interprets your walking as weakness, say: "This is my proven strategy for a strong finish."
- Even if you are pushing fairly hard, enjoy the race as much as possible, smile often.
- On warm days, pour water over your head at the start, possibly wetting your running top.

## After mid-race

- When the going gets tough, do everything you can to relax, and keep the muscles resilient.
- Keep going—tell yourself this over and over during the tough moments. Shorten the stride and pick up turnover.

- During the last half mile, don't let your legs slow down. One more step! Success is not letting up. You can do it!

## At the finish

- In the upright position
- With a smile on your face
- Wanting to do it again

## After the finish

- Keep walking for at least a quarter of a mile.
- Drink about 4-8 oz. of fluid.
- Within 30 min of the finish, have a snack that is 80% carbohydrate/20% protein (Endurox R4 is best).
- If you can soak your legs in cool water during the first two hours after the race, do so.
- Walk for 20-30 minutes later in the day.

## The next day

- Walk for 30-60 minutes, very easy. This can be done at one time, or in installments.
- Keep drinking about 4-6 oz. an hour of water or a sports drink like Accelerade.
- Wait at least a week before you either schedule your next race, or vow to never run another one again.

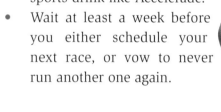

# Looking for a good 5K?

## Where to find out about races

### Running stores

This resource is at the top of our list because you can usually get entry forms, plus some editorial comment about the race. Explain to the store folks what you want to do in the race (competition for a certain time), etc. They will probably ask you for your projected finish time (or goal time). They'll look over the race choices to find a race that should have a good number of people to pull you along at that pace.

### Friends who run

Call a friend who has run for several years. Tell him or her that you are looking for a race that is well organized, and accurately measured. Be sure to ask the friend for a contact number or website where you can find more information on the event, and possibly enter. As with running store folks, the editorial comments and evaluation of an event can steer you to a good experience.

### Running clubs

If there is a running club or two in your area, get in touch. The officers or members can help you "match up" with an event for your time goal. Running clubs may be found by doing a web search: type "running clubs (your town)." The RRCA (Road Runner's Club of America) is a national organization of neighborhood clubs. From their website, search for a club in your area.

*Newspaper listings*

In many newspapers, there is a listing of community sports events in the weekend section. This comes out on Friday or Saturday in most cities, usually in the lifestyle section. Some listings can be in the sports section under "running" or "road races." You can often find these listings on the website of the local newspaper.

*Web searches*

Just do a web search for "road races (your town)" or "5K (your town)." There are several event companies that serve as a registration center for many races: including www.signmeup.com or www.active.com. From these sites you can sometimes find an event in your area, research it, and then sign up.

## How to register

1. Online. More and more of the road running events are conducting registration online. This allows you to bypass the process of finding an entry form. It becomes easier to enter before the deadline.

2. Fill out an entry and send it in. You will need to fill out your name, address, T-shirt size, etc., and then sign the waiver form. Be sure to include a check for the entry fee.

3. Show up on race day. Because some races don't do race day registration, be sure that you can do this. There is usually a penalty for waiting until the last minute, but you can see what the weather is like before you make the trek to the race.

# MENTAL TOUGHNESS

*"You can gain control over your attitude through mental training."*

The choice is yours. You can take control over your attitude, or you can let outside factors take you on a motivational roller coaster: fired up one day, and down the next. Whether you struggle to get out the door when starting a program, or you cannot stay motivated, you will find yourself on track more often when you have a strategy—a motivational training program. To understand the process, we must first look inside your head.

The brain has two hemispheres that are separated and don't interconnect. The logical left brain does our business activities, trying to steer us into pleasure and away from discomfort. The creative and intuitive right side is an unlimited source of solutions to problems, and connects us to hidden strengths.

As we accumulate stress, the left brain sends us a stream of messages, telling us to "slow down," "stop and you'll feel better," "this isn't your day," and even philosophical messages like "why are you doing this." We are all capable of staying on track, and even pushing to a higher level of performance, even when the left brain, is saying these things. So the first important step in taking command over motivation is to ignore the left brain unless there is a legitimate reason of health or safety (very rare), or the reality that you are running a lot faster than you are ready to run. You can deal with the left brain through a series of mental training drills.

These drills allow the right side of the brain to work on solutions to current problems. As the negative messages spew out of the left brain, the right brain doesn't argue. By preparing mentally for the challenges you expect, you will empower the right brain to deal with the problems and to develop mental toughness. Meanwhile the body gets the job done. But even more important, you will have three strategies for success.

## Drill #1

# Rehearsing success

### Getting out the door after a hard day

By rehearsing yourself through a motivation problem, you can be more consistent and set the stage to improve. You must first have a goal that is do-able, and a rehearsal situation that is realistic. Let's learn by doing:

1. State your desired outcome: to be running from my house after a hard day.

2. Detail the challenge: low blood sugar and fatigue, a stream of negative messages, need to get the evening meal ready to be cooked, overwhelming desire to feel relaxed.

3. Break up the challenge into a series of actions which lead you through the mental barriers, no one of which is challenging to the left brain.

- You're driving home at the end of the day, knowing that it is your workout day but you have no energy.
- Your left brain says: "You're too tired," "take the day off," "you don't have the energy to run."
- So you say to the left brain: "I'm not going to exercise. I'll put on some comfortable shoes and clothes, eat and drink, get food preparation going for dinner, and feel relaxed."
- You're in your room, putting on comfortable clothes and shoes (they just happen to be used for running).
- You're drinking coffee (tea, diet cola, etc.) and eating a good tasting energy snack as you get the food prepared to go into the oven.
- Stepping outside, you check on the weather.
- You're walking to the edge of your block to see what the neighbors are doing.
- As you cross the street, you're on your way.
- The endorphins are kicking in, you feel good, and you want to continue.

4. Rehearse the situation over and over, fine-tuning it so that it becomes integrated into the way you think and act, and it reflects the specific situation that you will encounter in your race.

5. Finish by mentally enjoying the good feelings experienced with the desired outcome. You have felt the good attitude, the vitality, the glow from a good run-walk, and you are truly relaxed. So, revisit these positive feelings at the end of each rehearsal.

## Getting out the door early in the morning

The second most common motivational problem that I'm asked about relates to the comfort of the bed, when you wake up and know that it is time to run.

State your desired outcome: to be walking and running away from the house early in the morning.

Detail the challenge: Desire to lie in bed, no desire to exert yourself so early. The stress of the alarm clock, and having to think about what to do next when the brain isn't working very fast.

Break up the challenge into a series of actions, which lead you through the mental barriers, no one of which is challenging to the left brain.

• The night before, lay out your running clothes and shoes, near your coffee pot, so that you don't have to think.
• Set your alarm, and say to yourself over and over, "feet on the floor, alarm off, to the coffee pot." Or...."floor, alarm, coffee." As you repeat this, you visualize doing each action without thinking. By repeating it, you lull yourself to sleep. You have been programming yourself for taking action the next morning.
• The alarm goes off. You put the feet on the floor, shut the alarm off, and head to the coffee pot—all without thinking.

- You're putting on one piece of clothing at a time, sipping coffee, never thinking about exercise.
- With coffee cup in hand, you walk out the door to see what the weather is like.
- Sipping coffee, you walk to the edge of your block or property to see what the neighbors are doing.
- Putting coffee down, you cross the street, and you have made the break!
- The endorphins are kicking in, you feel good, you want to continue.

*Rehearsals* develop patterns of thinking that get you in the groove for the behaviors you need to do. In a challenging situation, you don't want to have to think about the stress or the challenge, but instead, take action: move from one behavior to the next. The power of the rehearsal is that you have formatted your brain for a series of actions so that you don't have to think, and the sequence becomes almost automatic. By repeating the pattern, you'll revise it for real life, and become the successful runner you want to be!

## Pushing past the fatigue point where you tend to slow down

You're into a hard workout or race, and you are really tired. Your left brain is telling you that you can't reach your goal today, "just slow down a little, there are other days to work hard."

Evaluate whether there is a real medical reason why you can't run as projected. If there is a reason, back off and conserve—there will be another day.

Almost every time, however, the problem is more simple: you are not willing to push through the discomfort. The most effective way of getting tough mentally is to gradually push back your limits. Speed training programs can help you greatly. As you add to the number of repetitions each week, you'll work on the mind as the body gets all systems working together to run faster.

Don't quit! Mental toughness can be as simple as not giving up. Just ignore the negative messages, and stay focused to the finish. If you've trained adequately, hang on and keep going.

In your speed workouts, practice the following drill. Fine-tune this so that when you run your goal race, you will have a strategy for staying mentally tough.

## The scene
You're getting very tired, you'd really like to call it quits, or at least slow down significantly.

## Quick strategies
- Break up the remaining workout or race into segments that you know you can do:
  *"1 more minute":* Run for one minute, then reduce pace slightly for 10 seconds, then say "1 more minute" again, and again.
  *"10 more steps":* Run about 10 steps, take a couple of easy steps, then say "ten more steps."
  *"One more step":* Keep saying this over and over—you'll get there.

## Take some shuffle breaks
- Reduce the tension on your leg muscles and feet by shuffling for a few strides every 1-2 minutes. By practicing "the shuffle," you'll find that you don't slow down much at all, while your muscles feel better.

## Lap by lap, mile by mile

- In the workouts, start each lap saying to yourself—"just one more" (even if you have 4 to go), or "I'll just run half a lap." You'll run the whole thing.

- In a track race, say "one more lap," or "one more half lap," or "just around the curve." In a road race, say "one more mile," "one more block," "just around the curve."

- When you are getting close to the end and really feel like you can't keep going, say to yourself "I am tough," or "I can endure," or "Yes I can."

## Drill # 2

# Magic words

Even the most motivated person has sections during a tough workout or race when they want to quit. By using a successful brainwashing technique, you can pull yourself through these negative thoughts, and feel like a champion at the end. On these days you have not only reached the finish line, you've overcome challenges to get there.

Think back to the problems that you face in your tough workouts or races. These are the ones that are most likely to challenge you again. As you go through a series of speed sessions and long runs, you will go through just about every problem you will face. Go back in your memory bank, and pull out instances when you started to lose motivation due to these, but finished and overcame the challenge.

In really tough runs, I have three challenges that occur over and over:

**1)** I become tense when I get really tired, worried that I will struggle badly at the end.

**2)** I feel the loss of the bounce and strength I had at the beginning, and worry that there will be no strength at the end.

**3)** My form starts to get ragged, and I worry about further deterioration of muscles and tendons and more fatigue due to "wobbling."

Over the past three decades I have learned to counter these three problems with the magic words "Relax... Power.... Glide." The visualization of each of these positives helps a little. The real magic comes from the association I have made with hundreds of successful experiences when I started to "lose it" in one of the three areas, but overcame the problems. Each time I "run through" one or more of the problems, I associate the experience with these magic words and add to the magic.

Now, when something starts to go wrong, I repeat the three words, over and over. Instead of increasing my anxiety, the repetition of the words calms me down. Even though I don't feel as strong at lap 5 as I did at lap 1, I'm empowered just by knowing that I have a strategy and can draw upon my past experience. And when my legs lose the efficient path and bounce, I make adjustments and keep going.

When I say magic words that are associated with successful experience, there are two positive effects. The saying of the words floods the brain with positive memories. For a while, the negative messages of the left brain don't have a chance, and you can get down the track for a lap or two. But the second effect may be more powerful. The words directly link you to the right brain, which works intuitively to make the same connections that allowed you solve the problems before.

To be successful on any day, you only need to finish the race. Most of the time you can get through the "bad parts" by not giving up, and simply putting one foot in front of the other. As you push beyond the negative left brain messages, you create the confidence to do this again, and again. Feel free to use my magic words, or develop your own. The more experiences you have associated with the words, the more magic they have.

## Dirty tricks

The strategy of the rehearsal drill will get you focused and organized, while reducing the stress for the first few miles. Magic words will pull you along through most of the rest of the challenging sessions. But on the really rough days, it helps to have some dirty tricks to play on the left side of the brain.

These are quick fixes that distract the left brain for a while, allowing you to get down the road or the track for 300 yards or more. These imaginative and sometimes crazy images don't have to have any logic behind them. But when you counter a left brain message with a creative idea, you confuse the left brain and stop the flow of negative messages.

# The giant invisible rubber band

When I get tired on long or hard runs, I unpack this secret weapon, and throw it around someone ahead of me—or someone who had the audacity to pass me. For a while, the person doesn't realize that he or she has been "looped," and continues to push onward while I get the benefit of being pulled along. After a minute or two of mentally projecting myself into this image, I have to laugh for believing in such an absurd notion. But laughing activates the creative right side of the brain. This usually generates several more entertaining ideas, especially when you do this on a regular basis.

The right brain has millions of dirty tricks. Once you get it activated, you are likely to experience its solutions to problems you are currently having. It can entertain you as you get closer to your finish, step-by-step.

For many more dirty tricks and mental strategies, see *Galloway's Book on Running* and *Marathon —You Can Do It*.

# EATING FOR PERFORMANCE

There are a few foods that, when eaten at the right time, can help you run a better workout, be more motivated during a race, and recover faster. There are a lot more foods, however, that can reduce your performance, and cause problems. In this part of the book, you'll learn that "what not to eat" is at least as important as the foods that give you nutrition.

## Maintaining blood sugar level

The blood sugar level (BSL) determines how good you feel: how motivated you will be to exercise, to race, and to keep going at the end of a hard run. When it is at a good, moderate level—for you—you feel energized, stable and motivated. If you eat too much sugar in food or drink, however, your BSL can rise too high. You'll feel really good for a while, but the excess sugar triggers a release of insulin, that usually pushes it too low. In this lowered state (about 30-60 minutes after a sugar snack) you don't have energy, mental focus is foggy, and motivation goes down rapidly.

When blood sugar level is maintained throughout the day, you will not only have an energetic feeling about workouts—you'll want to add other energy and activity to your life. You'll have a more positive mental attitude, and be more likely to deal with stress and solve problems. The steady infusion of balanced nutrients all day long will maintain stable blood sugar.

You don't want to get on the "bad side" of your BSL. Low levels are a stress on the system and literally mess with your mind. Your brain is fed by blood sugar, and when the supply goes down, your mental stress goes up. If you have not eaten for several hours before a run, your left brain will tell you that you don't have the energy to exercise, that it will hurt, and other unmotivating thoughts. Low BSL will also decrease your enjoyment and energy level during a run, making it more difficult to power the muscles for quality speed repetitions.

It is best to keep a snack with you all day as a BSL insurance policy. Eating blood sugar boosters every 2 hours or so, can often be the difference whether you get out and run that day or not. But there's still hope up until 30 minutes before your run. You can turn a low BSL around at that point by eating a snack that has 80% carbohydrate and 20% protein.

## The BSL roller coaster

Eating a snack with too many calories of simple carbohydrate can be counter-productive for BSL maintenance. As mentioned above, when the sugar level gets too high, your body produces insulin, sending BSL lower than before. The tendency is to eat again, which produces excess calories that are converted into fat.

But if you don't eat, you'll stay hungry, miserable, and not in a mood to spend any energy—not to mention the strenuous demands of a hard speed session.

## Eating every 2-3 hours is best

Once you find which snacks work best to maintain your BSL, most people maintain a stable blood sugar level better by eating small meals regularly, every 2-3 hours.  It's best to combine complex carbs with protein and a small amount of fat. After talking to a number of highly respected dieticians and biochemists, here is a guide for the composition of the snacks:

### Composition of snacks to help you feel satisfied:

(expressed as a percentage of the total calories of that snack)

| | |
|---|---|
| Fat: | 15-25% |
| Protein: | 20-30% |
| Complex carbohydrate: | 35-60% |
| Simple carbohydrate | 5-10% |

Nutrients that leave you satisfied longer after a snack or meal:

*Fat*

Fat will leave you satisfied from a small meal because it slows down digestion. But a little goes a long way. When the fat content of a meal goes beyond 30%, you'll feel increasingly more lethargic due to the fact that fat is harder to digest. So it helps to eat a little fat, but a lot of it will lead to sluggishness.

*Protein*—lean protein is best.

This nutrient is needed every day for rebuilding the muscle that is broken down continuously, as well as normal wear and tear. Runners, even those who log high mileage, don't need to eat significantly more protein than sedentary people. But, if runners don't get their usual amount of protein, they feel more aches and pains, and general tiredness sooner than average people.

Having protein with each meal will leave you feeling satisfied (in terms of blood sugar level) for a longer period of time. But more is not necessarily better: eating more protein calories than you need will result in a conversion of the excess into fat.

Recently, protein has been added to sports drinks with great success. When a drink with 80% carbohydrate and 20% protein (such as Accelerade) is consumed within 30 minutes of the start of a run, glycogen is activated better, and energy is supplied sooner and better. The same drink during a long speed workout can help you recover between repetitions (usually 2-4 oz.). Consuming a 80%-20% drink after a hard run (like Endurox R4) within 30 minutes after finishing can speed recovery.

*Complex carbohydrates* give you a "discount" and a "grace period.

Foods, such as celery, beans, cabbage, spinach, turnip greens, grape nuts, course whole grain bread, etc., are so gritty or fibrous that up to 25% of the calories are burned in the digestion of the food. As opposed to fat (which is directly deposited on your body after eating it), it is only the excess carbs that are processed into fat. After dinner (the grace period) you have the opportunity to burn off any excess that you acquired during the day. The complexity of the fibers and the grains, eaten in a small meal during the day, leaves you satisfied longer due to a longer period of time needed to digest them. But eating too much whole grain cereal, for example, right before exercising, can lead to nausea and carbohydrate un-loading.

### *Fat + Protein + Complex Carbs = SATISFACTION*
Eating a snack that has a variety of the three satisfaction ingredients above, will lengthen the time that you'll feel satisfied, even after some very small meals. These three items take longer to digest, and therefore keep the metabolism rate revved up.

## Other important nutrients...

### *Vitamins and minerals*
A runner who is testing his limits in speedwork, may be surprised to find that you don't need significantly more vitamins and minerals, protein, etc. than a sedentary person. But if you don't get these ingredients for several days in a row, you will feel the effects when you try to exercise.

The **B vitamin** complex is needed for energy production, and to help manage the free radicals produced by exercise. This group of vitamins has also been shown to help prevent the production of harmful substances that have been involved in heart disease, alzheimers, and other negative health problems.

**Vitamin C** speeds up healing and the production of connective tissue. It is also an anti-oxidant.

***Vitamin E*** has been shown to be an anti-oxidant with many healthy benefits. There is some conflicting research on vitamin E.

***Iron*** is needed for production of the red blood cells, which carry oxygen to the muscle cells. Since you lose a little iron with each drop of sweat, make sure that you are getting some iron every day. One of the best sources of iron is cooking your food in an iron skillet.

### Fiber

When fiber is put into foods, it slows down digestion and maintains the feeling of satisfaction longer. Soluable fiber, such as oat bran, seems to bestow a longer feeling of satisfaction than unsoluable fiber, such as wheat bran. But any type of fiber will help in this regard. Fiber promotes the use of the muscles in the intestine, which helps to move the food through the digestive tract.

### Water: The most important nutrient

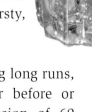

Whether you drink water, juice, sports drinks, diet drinks, etc., drink regularly throughout the day 6-8 oz. every 1-2 hours. Under normal circumstances, your thirst is a good guide for fluid consumption. I will not tell you that you must drink 8 glasses of water a day, because I've not seen any research to back this up. Fluid researchers who follow this topic tell me that if we drink regularly (every 2 hours or so) and when thirsty, fluid levels are maintained at necessary levels.

If you are having to take bathroom stops during long runs, you are probably drinking too much—either before or during the exercise. During an exercise session of 60 minutes or less, most runners don't need to drink at all. The intake of fluid before exercise should be arranged so that the excess fluid is eliminated before the run. Each person is a bit different, so you will have to find the right quantity and routine that works for you.

## Do I have to eat before running?

Most people who run in the morning don't need to eat anything before the start. As mentioned above, if your blood sugar level is low in the afternoon, and you have a run scheduled, a snack can help when taken about 30 minutes before the run. If you feel that a morning snack will help, the only issue is to avoid consuming so much that you get an upset stomach.

### Drinking/Eating schedule before a hard morning run

- 1 hour before a morning run: either a cup of coffee or a glass of water. If you need to eat something, have half of an energy bar or a packet of GU or a gel packet.
- 30 min before any run (if blood sugar is low and you have not had any food) 100 calories of a drink that has 80% carbohydrate and 20% protein
- Within 30 min after a run: 200 calories of a 80% carb/20% protein (Endurox R4, for example)
- If you are sweating a lot during hot weather, 3-4 glasses of a good electrolyte beverage like Accelerade, throughout the day

## Get insulin working for you

For best results in raising blood sugar when it is too low (within 30 minutes before a run), a snack should have about 80% of the calories in simple carbohydrate and 20% in protein. This promotes the production of insulin, which is helpful before a run in processing the carbohydrate into a form (glycogen) that the muscles can use very quickly. The product Accelerade has worked best among the thousands of runners I hear from every year. It has the 80%/20% ratio of carb to protein. If you eat an energy bar with the 80/20 ratio, be sure to drink 6-8 oz. of water or coffee with it. Many runners consume an energy bar (or half an energy bar) about an hour before exercise.

## Eating during exercise

Most exercisers don't need to worry about eating or drinking during a run. In fact, the body shuts down in its ability to process almost anything, and eating even sports nutrition products can make you nauseous. But when your slow long runs exceed 90 minutes, the blood sugar level starts to drop. At this point, there are several options listed below. Most runners find it productive to start taking the food product about 40 minutes into the workout. This helps when running long, or during a long track session.

GU or gel products—these come in small packets, and are the consistency of honey or thick syrup. The most successful way to take them is to put the contents of 1-2 packets in a small plastic bottle with a pop-top. About every 10-15 minutes, take a small squirt with a sip or two of water.

*Energy Bars*—Cut into 8-10 pieces and take a piece, with a couple of sips of water, every 10-15 minutes.

*Candy*—particularly gummi bears or hard candies. The usual consumption is 1-2 pieces, about every 10 minutes.

*Sports Drinks*—Since nausea is experienced by a significant number of those who drink these products during exercise, I'm not going to recommend them. If you have had success when using sports drinks in workouts or races, drink it in the same quantity, and on the same schedule as you have used it before.

Exception: during your rest interval, when doing speed repetitions, a slightly diluted sports drink like Accelerade has helped maintain BSL, and speeded recovery, according to research.

## It is important to re-load after exercise—within 30 minutes

Whenever you have finished a hard or long workout (for you), a reloading snack of about 200-300 calories will help you recover faster. Again, the 80/20 ratio of carb to protein has been most successful in replenishing the glycogen stores into the muscle cells. The product that has worked best for the thousands of runners I work with each year is Endurox R4.

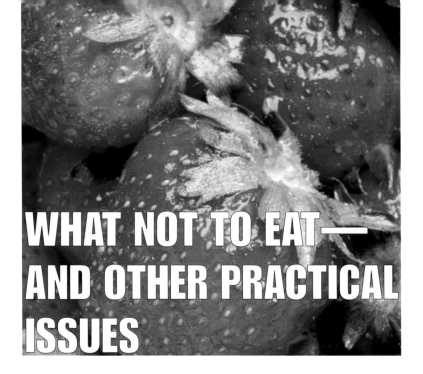

# WHAT NOT TO EAT— AND OTHER PRACTICAL ISSUES

**M**ost of the nutritional problems that I hear about are due to eating too much, ingesting too soon before running, or consuming the wrong foods. While there are many individual differences in all of the eating variables, it's always better to err on the side of eating less the closer you get to the workout or race.

## Practical eating issues

* You don't need to eat before a run, unless your blood sugar is low (see the previous chapter).
* Reload most effectively by eating within 30 min of the finish of a run (80% carb/20% protein). Avoid fat within 90 minutes of the finish of a hard run.
* Eating or drinking too much right before the start of a run will interfere with deep breathing, and may cause

side pain. The food or fluid in your stomach limits your intake of air into the lower lungs, and restricts the diaphragm, causing the pain in area just below the ribs.

- If you are running low on blood sugar at the end of your long runs or long workouts, take some blood sugar booster with you (see the previous chapter for suggestions).

- It is never a good idea to eat a huge meal. Those who claim that they must "carbo load" are often rationalizing the desire to eat a lot of food. Eating a big meal the night before (or the day of) a race, or before a hard workout or a long run can be a real problem. The food will require an extensive blood flow to the gut, depriving the exercising muscles of this precious fluid. In addition, you will have a lot of food in your gut as you bounce up and down for an extended period. This could get ugly.

- A radical change in the foods you eat is not a good idea, and usually leads to problems, especially within 12 hours before a hard workout or race.

## The bad side of fat

There are two kinds of fat that have been found to cause narrowing of the arteries around the heart and leading to your brain: saturated fat and trans fat. Mono and un-saturated fats, from vegetable sources, are often healthy—olive oil, nuts, avocado, safflower oil. Some fish oils have Omega 3 fatty acids, which have been shown to have a protective effect on the heart. Many fish, however, have oil that is not protective.

Look carefully at the labels, because a lot of foods have vegetable oils that have been processed into trans fat. A wide range of baked goods and other foods have this unhealthy substance. It helps to check the labels. Since labels are often confusing, call the 800 number to check on the kind of fat in this case. Your other choice is to avoid the food.

## When to watch water intake

During extremely long runs of over 4 hours, medical experts from major marathons recommend no more than 27 oz. an hour of fluid. Most folks need less than this. For most runners, this means drinking about 4 oz. (half a glass) every 1-2 miles.

## Sweat the electrolytes

Electrolytes are the salts that your body loses when you sweat: sodium, potassium, magnesium and calcium. When you have not restocked your supply of these, your fluid transfer system doesn't work as well and you may experience ineffective cooling, muscle cramps (see the next chapter), and other problems. Most runners have no problem replacing these in a normal diet, but if you are experiencing cramping during or after exercise regularly, you may be low in sodium or potassium. The best product I've found for replacing these minerals is called SUCCEED. If you have high blood pressure, a mineral imbalance, etc., get your doctor's guidance before taking any salt supplement.

When you are sweating a lot, it is a good idea to drink several glasses a day of a good electrolyte beverage. Accelerade, by Pacific Health Labs, is the best I've seen for both maintaining fluid levels and electrolyte levels.

# CROSS TRAINING: GETTING BETTER AS YOU REST THE LEGS

*"Alternative exercise allows runners to rest the running muscles while getting their exercise fix."*

The best item you can insert into a speed training program to reduce injury is an extra rest day or two. The hard work of running involves lifting your body off the ground, and then absorbing the shock. If you are doing this every other day—even running fast—the limited damage can be repaired, and your fitness improved. Many runners—even in their 50s and 60s don't ever have injury layoffs when running every other day.

Once runners get into a speed program, and start to improve, some will try to sneak in an extra day or two on the days they should be "off." They often feel, mistakenly, that they can gain performance with an additional day; or that they are losing fitness when they take a day off. This is not a match-up with reality. Even with easy and short runs (on days that should be off), the legs cannot fully recover—especially from speed workouts. These short runs on rest days are the so-called "junk miles."

## Cross training activities

The middle ground is to run one day, and cross train the next. Cross training simply means "alternative exercise" to running. Your goal is to find exercises that give you a good feeling of exertion, but without tiring the workhorses of running: calf muscles, Achilles tendon, feet.

The other exercises may not deliver the same good feelings—but they can come close. Many runners report that it may take a combination of 3 or 4 segments in a session to do this. But even if you don't feel exactly the same way, you'll receive the relaxation that comes from exercise while you burn calories and fat.

### When you are starting to do any exercise (or starting back, after a layoff):

1. Start with 5 easy minutes of exercise, rest for 20 or more minutes, and do 5 more easy minutes.
2. Take a day of rest between this exercise (you can do a different exercise the next day).
3. Increase by 2-3 additional minutes each session, until you get to the number of minutes that gives you the appropriate feeling of exertion.

4. Once you have reached two 15 minute sessions, you could shift to one 22-25 minute session, and increase by 2-3 more minutes per session if you wish.

5. It's best to do no exercise the day before a long run—or a very hard speed session, or race.

6. To maintain your conditioning in each alternative exercise, do one session a week of 10 minutes or more once your reach that amount.

7. The maximum cross training is up to the individual. As long as you are feeling fine for the rest of the day, and are having no trouble with your runs, the length of your cross training should not be a problem.

## Water running can improve your running form

All of us have little flips and side motions of our legs that interfere with our running efficiency. During a water running workout, the resistance of the water forces your legs to find a more efficient path. In addition, several leg muscles are strengthened which can help to keep your legs on a smoother path when they get tired at the end of a long run.

*Here's how!*

You'll need a flotation belt for this exercise. The product "aqua jogger" is designed to float you off the bottom of the pool, and on most runners tightens, so that it is close to the body. There are many other ways to keep you floating, including simple ski float belts and life jackets.

Get in the deep end of the pool and move your legs through a running motion. This means little or no knee lift, kicking out slightly in front of you, and bringing the leg behind, with the foot coming up behind you. As in running, your lower leg should be parallel with the horizontal during the back-kick.

If you are not feeling much exertion, you're probably lifting the knees too high and moving your legs through a tiny range of motion. To get the benefit, an extended running motion is needed.

It's important to do water running once a week to keep the adaptations that you have gained. If you miss a week, you should drop back a few minutes from your previous session. If you miss more than 3 weeks, start back at two 5-8 min sessions.

## Fat burning and overall fitness exercises

*Nordic track*

This exercise machine simulates the motion used in cross country skiing. It is one of the better cross training modes for fat burning, because it allows you to use a large number of muscle cells while raising body temperature. If you exercise at an easy pace, you can get into the fat burning zone (past 45 minutes) after a gradual build-up to that amount. This exercise requires no pounding of the legs or feet, and (unless you push it too hard or too long) allows you to run as usual the next day.

### Rowing machine

There are a number of different types of rowing machines. Some work the legs a bit too hard for runners, but most allow you to use a wide variety of lower and upper body muscle groups. Like nordic track, if you have the right machine for you, it's possible to continue to exercise for about as long as you wish once you have gradually worked up to this. Most of the better machines will use a large number of muscle cells, raise temperature, and can be continued for more than three-quarters of an hour.

### Cycling

Indoor cycling (on an exercise cycle) is a better fat burner exercise than outdoor cycling, because it raises your body temperature more—you don't get the cooling effect of the breeze that you generate on a bike. The muscles used in both indoor and outdoor cycling are mostly the quadriceps muscles—on the front of the upper thigh— reducing the total number of muscle cells compared with water running, nordic track, etc.

### Don't forget walking!

Walking can be done all day long. I call walking a "stealth fat-burner" exercise because it is so easy to walk mile after mile—especially in small doses. But it is also an excellent cross training exercise. This includes walking on the treadmill. Caution: Don't walk with a long stride.

## Cross training for the upper body

### Weight training

While weight work is not a great fat-burning exercise, and does not directly benefit running, it can be done on non-running days, or on running days after a run. There is a wide range of different ways to build strength. If interested, find a coach that can help you build strength in the muscle groups you wish. As mentioned previously in this book, weight training for the legs is not recommended.

## Swimming

While not a fat-burner, swimming strengthens the upper body while improving cardiovascular fitness and endurance in those muscles. Swimming can be done on both running days and non-running days.

## Push-ups and pull-ups

These can build great upper body strength as you innovate to work the upper body muscle groups you want to strengthen. If interested, see a strength expert for these variations.

### Don't do these on non-running days!

The following exercises will tire the muscles used for running and keep them from recovering between running days. If you really like to do any of these exercises, you can do them after a run, on a running day.

- Stair machines
- Stair aerobics
- Weight training for the leg muscles
- Power walking—especially on a hilly course
- Spinning classes (on a bicycle) in which you get out of your seat

# Cross training can keep you fit if you must stop running

I know of many runners who have had to take 2 weeks off from running or more, and have not lost noticeable fitness. How? They cross trained.

As noted above, the most effective cross training mode is water running. I've known runners at a wide range of abilities that have maintained speed and marathon conditioning during several weeks off from running.

The key is to do an activity (like water running) that uses the same range of motion used in running. This keeps the neuromuscular system working to capacity.

To maintain conditioning, you must simulate the time and the effort level you would have spent when running. For example, if you were scheduled for a long run that would have taken you 60 minutes, get in the pool and run for 60 minutes. You can take segments of 30-40 seconds in which you reduce your effort (like a walk break), every few minutes, to keep the muscles resilient.

On a speed day, run water segments of about the same time you would have run for those segments on the track. Whether going long or fast, try to get up to the same approximate respiration rate that you would have felt when running.

# TOOLS: HEART MONITORS AND GPS DEVICES

## Heart monitors

Left brain runners who are motivated by technical items and data tracking tell me that they are more motivated when using a heart monitor. Right brain runners who love the intuitive feel of running find that the after-workout number crunching is too intense, jolting them out of their mindset of transcendental running. But after talking with hundreds of both types of runners, I realize that there are benefits—especially for runners who are doing speed training.

Once you determine your maximum heart rate, a good heart monitor can help you manage your effort level. This will give you more control over the amount of effort you are spending in a workout, so that you can reduce overwork and recovery time. As they push into the exertion zone needed on a hard workout, left brain runners will gain a reasonably accurate reading on how much effort to spend, or how much they need to back off to avoid a long recovery. Many "type A" runners feel that the monitors pay for themselves by telling them exactly how slow to run on easy days, and during rest intervals during workouts. Right brain runners admit that they enjoy getting verification of their intuitive evaluation of effort levels. The bottom line is that monitors can tell you to go slow enough to recover, and not too fast on the hard days.

All devices have their "technical difficulties." Heart monitors can be influenced by local electronic transmissions and mechanical issues. Cell phone towers and even garage doors can interfere with a monitor on occasion. This is usually an incidental issue. But if you have an abnormal reading, either high or low, it may be a technical abnormality.

Be sure to read the instruction manual thoroughly—particularly about how to attach the device for best reading. If not attached securely, you will miss some beats. This means that you are actually working a lot harder than you think you are.

I suggest that you keep monitoring how you feel, at each 5% percentage increase toward the maximum heart rate (max heart rate). Over time, you will get better at telling when you are at 85% when you should be at 80%.

### Get tested to determine max heart rate

If you are going to use a heart monitor, you should be tested to find your maximum heart rate. Some doctors (especially cardiologists) will do this. Other testing facilities include Human Performance Labs at Universities, and some health clubs and YMCAs. It is best to have someone supervising the test who is trained in cardiovascular issues. Sometimes the testing facility will misunderstand what you want. Be sure to say that you only need a "max heart rate test"—not a maximum oxygen uptake test. Once you have run for a couple of months with the monitor, you will have a clear idea what your max heart rate is from looking at your heart rate during a series of hard runs. Even on the hard speed workouts, you can usually sense whether you could have worked yourself harder. But until you have more runs that push you to the limits, assume that your current top heart rate is within a beat or three of your max. This is another safeguard that will help you avoid overtraining.

### Use the percentage of max heart rate as your standard

You don't want to get to even 90% of max heart rate during most workouts. At the end of a long training program, this may happen at the end of a workout or two. But your goal is to keep the percentage between 70% and 80% during the first half of the workout or longer, and minimize the upward drift at the end of the workout.

### Computing max heart rate percentage

For example, if your max heart rate is 200:

90% is 180
80% is 160
70% is 140
65% is 130

### On easy days, stay below 65% of max heart rate

When in doubt, run slower. One of the major reasons for fatigue, aches and pains and burnout is not running slowly enough on the recovery and fun days. Most commonly, the rate will increase at the end of a run. If this happens, slow down and take more walk breaks to keep it below 65%.

### Between speed repetitions, let the pulse rate drop to 65% of max before doing another rep

To reduce the "lingering fatigue" that may continue for days after a hard workout, extend the rest interval walk until the heart rate goes down to this 65% level or lower. At the end of the workout, if the heart rate does not drop below this level for 5 minutes, you should do your warm down and call it a day.

### Run smoother on speed repetitions, so that your heart rate stays below 80% during speedwork

If you really work on running form improvements, you can minimize the heart rate increase by running more efficiently: keeping the feet low to the ground, using a light touch, maintaining a quick but efficient turnover of the feet. For more info on this, see the "Running Form" chapter in this book, or *Galloway's Book on Running*.

### Morning pulse

If the chest strap doesn't interfere with your sleep, you can get a very accurate reading on your resting pulse in the morning. This will allow you to monitor over-training. Record the low figures each night. Once you establish a baseline, you should take an easy day when the rate rises 5%-9% above this. When it reaches 10% or above, you should take an extra day off. Even if the heart rate increase is due to an infection, You should not run unless cleared by your doctor.

*Use the "two minute rule" for the pace of long runs—not heart rate*

Even when running at 65% of max heart rate, many runners will be running a lot faster than they should at the beginning of long runs. Read the guidelines in this book for pacing the long runs, and don't be bashful about running slower.

*But at the end of long runs, back off when heart rate exceeds 70% of max*

There will be some upward drift of heart rate, due to fatigue at the end of long runs. Keep slowing down if this happens, so that you stay around 70% of max HR, or lower.

## GPS and other distance/pace calculators

There are two types of devices for measuring distance, and both are usually very accurate:  GPS  and accelerometer technology. While some devices are more accurate than others, most will tell you almost exactly how far you have run. This provides the best pacing feedback I know of— except for running on a track.

Using the more accurate products gives you freedom. You can do your long runs without having to measure the course, or being forced to run on a repeated, but measured loop. Instead of going to a track to do speed sessions, you can very quickly measure your segments on roads, trails, or residential streets with GPS devices. If your goal race is on the track, I recommend that at least half of your speed sessions be run on the track. This relates to the principle of training called "specificity."

The GPS devices track your movements by the use of navigational satellites. In general, the more satellites, the more accurate the measurement. There are "shadows" or areas of heavy trees or mountains in some areas where the signal cannot be acquired for (usually) short distances. You can see how accurate they are by running around a standard track. If you run in the second lane you will be running .25 mile.

The accelerometer products require a very easy calibration, and have also been shown to be very accurate. I've found it best on the calibration to use a variety of paces and a walk break or two in order to simulate what you will be doing when you run.

Some devices require batteries, and others can be re-charged. It helps to go to a technical running store for advice on these products. The staff there can often give you some "gossip" on the various brands and devices from the feedback they receive about how they work in real life.

# DEALING WITH THE HEAT

*"You're not going to run as fast
when the temperature rises."*

If you slow down a little on a warm day, you can finish strong, with a higher finish place. That seems obvious, but some runners "lose it" at the beginning of a hot race. The result is a much slower time, because of the inevitable slowdown at the end. For every second you run too fast during the first quarter mile of a race on a hot day, you can usually expect to run 2-10 seconds slower at the end.

When you exercise strenuously in high heat (above 75°F), or moderate heat (above 60°F) with high humidity (above 50%) you raise the core body temperature. Most beginning runners will see the internal temperature rise when outside temperature rises above 55°F. This triggers a release of blood into the capilliaries of your skin to help cool you down. This diversion reduces the blood supply available to your exercising muscles, meaning that you will have less blood and less oxygen delivered to the power source that moves you forward—and less blood to move out the waste products from these work sites. As the waste builds up in the muscle, you will slow down.

So the bad news is that in warm weather you are going to feel worse and run slower. The worse news is that working too hard on a hot day could result in a very serious condition called heat disease. Make sure that you read the section on this health problem at the end of this chapter. The good news is that you can adapt to these conditions to some extent, as you learn the best time of the day, clothing, and other tricks to keep you cool. But it is always better to back off or stop running at the first sign of this condition. The following are proven ways of avoiding heat adversity.

## Running the long workouts during summer heat

1.  Run before the sun gets above the horizon. Get up early during the warm months and you will avoid most of the dramatic stress from the sun. This is particularly a problem in humid areas. Early morning is usually the coolest time of the day, too. Without having to deal with the sun, most runners can gradually adapt to heat. At the very least, your runs will be more enjoyable. Note: be sure to take care of safety issues.

2. If you must run when the sun is up, pick a shady course. Shade provides a significant relief in areas of low humidity, and some relief in humid environments.

3. In areas of low humidity, it's usually cool during the evening and night. In humid environments there may not be much relief. The coolest time of the day when it's humid is just before dawn.

4. Have an indoor facility available. With treadmills, you can exercise in air conditioning. If a treadmill bores you, alternate segments of 5-10 minutes—one segment outdoor, and the next indoor.

5. Don't wear a hat! You lose most of your body heat through the top of your head. Covering the head will cause a quicker internal build-up of heat.

6. Wear light clothing, but not cotton. Many of the new, technical fibers (polypro, coolmax, drifit, etc.) will move moisture away from your skin, producing a cooling effect. Cotton soaks up the sweat, making the garment heavier as it sticks to your skin. This means that you won't receive as much of a cooling effect as that provided by the tech products.

7. Pour water over your head. Evaporation not only helps the cooling process, it makes you feel cooler. This offers a psychological boost which can be huge. If you can bring along ice water with you, you will feel a lot cooler as you squirt some regularly over the top of your head, using a pop top water bottle.

8. Do your short runs in installments. It is fine, on a hot day that is scheduled for an easy run, to put in your 30 minutes by doing 10 in the morning, 10 at noon and 10

at night. The long run, however, should be done at one time.

9.  Take a pool break, or a shower chill-down. During a run, it really helps to take a 2-4 minute dip in a pool or a shower. Some runners in hot areas run loops around their neighborhood, and let the hose run over the head each lap. The pool is especially helpful in soaking out excess body temperature. I have run in 97 degree temperatures at our Florida running retreat, breaking up a 5 mile run into 3 x 1.7 mile. Between each, I take a 2-3 minute "soak break," and get back out there. It was only at the end of each segment that I got warm again.

10. Sunscreen—a mixed review. Some runners will need to protect themselves. Some products, however, produce a coating on the skin, slowing down the perspiration and producing an increase in body temperature build-up. If you are only in the sun for 30-50 minutes at a time, you may not need to put on sunscreen for cancer protection. Consult with a dermatologist for your specific needs, or find a product that doesn't block the pores.

11. Drink 6-8 oz of a sports drink like Accelerade or water, at least every 2 hours, or when thirsty, throughout the day during hot weather.

12. Look at the clothing thermometer at the end of this section. Wear loose fitting garments, that have some texture in the fabric. Texture will limit or prevent the perspiration from causing a clinging and sticking to the skin.

13. When the temperature is above 90°F, you have my permission to re-arrange your running shoes—preferably in an air conditioned environment.

## Hot weather slowdown for long runs

As the temperature rises above 55°F, your body starts to build up heat, but most runners aren't significantly slowed until 60°F. If you make the adjustments early, you won't have to suffer later and slow down a lot more at that time. The baseline for this table is 60°F or 14°C.

| | |
|---|---|
| Between 60°F and 65°F Between 14°C and 17°C | slow down 30 seconds per mile slower than you would run at 60°F slow down 20 seconds per kilometer slower than you would run at 14°C |
| Between 66°F and 69°F Between 18°C and 19°C | Slow down one minute per mile slower than you would run at 60°F slow down 40 seconds per kilometer slower than you would run at 14°C |
| Between 70°F and 75°F Between 19°C and 22°C | slow down 1:30/mile slower than you would run at 60°F slow down one minute/kilometer slower than you would run at 14°C |
| Between 76°F and 80°F Between 23°C and 25°C | slow down 2 min./mi. slower than you would run at 60°F slow down 1:20/km slower than you would run at 14°C |
| Above 80°F and 25°C | be careful, take extra precautions to avoid heat disease Or....exercise indoors Or....arrange your shoes next to the air conditioner |

## Heat disease alert!

While it is unlikely that you will push yourself into heat disease, the longer you are exercising in hot (and/or humid) conditions, the more you increase the likelihood of this dangerous medical situation. That's why I recommend breaking up your exercise into short segments when it's hot, if you must run outdoors. Be sensitive to your reactions to the heat, and those of the runners around you. When one of the symptoms is present, this is normally not a major problem, unless there is significant distress. But when several are experienced, take action, because heat disease can lead to death. It's always better to be conservative: stop the workout and cool off.

## Symptoms:

- Intense heat build-up in the head
- General overheating of the body
- Significant headache
- Significant nausea
- General confusion and loss of concentration
- Loss of muscle control
- Excessive sweating and then cessation of sweating
- Clammy skin
- Excessively rapid breathing
- Muscle cramps
- Feeling faint
- Unusual heart beat or rhythm

## Risk factors:

- Viral or bacterial infection
- Taking medication—especially cold medicines, diruretics, medicines for diarrhea, antihistamines, atropine, scopolamine, tranquilizers, even cholesterol and blood pressure medications. Check with your

doctor on medication issues—especially when running in hot weather.

- Dehydration (especially due to alcohol)
- Severe sunburn
- Overweight
- Lack of heat training
- Exercising more than one is used to
- Occurrence of heat disease in the past
- Two or more nights of extreme sleep deprivation
- Certain medical conditions, including high cholesterol, high blood pressure, extreme stress, asthma, diabetes, epilepsy, cardiovascular disease, smoking, or a general lack of fitness
- Drug use, including alcohol, over-the-counter medications, prescription drugs, etc. (consult with your doctor about using drugs when you are exercising hard in hot weather)

## Take action! Call 911

Use your best judgement, but in most cases, anyone who exhibits two or more of the symptoms should get into a cool environment, and consult medical attention immediately. An extremely effective cool off method is to soak towels, sheets or clothing in cool or cold water, and wrap them around the individual. If ice is available, sprinkle some ice over the wet cloth.

### Heat adaptation workout

If you regularly force yourself to deal with body heat build-up, your body will get better at running closer to your potential when hot. As with all training components, it is important to do this regularly. You should be sweating to some extent at the end of the workout, although the amount and the duration of perspiration is an individual issue. If the heat is particularly difficult, cut back the amount. Don't let yourself get into the beginning stages of heat disease. Get the doctor's clearance before doing this.

## Important Note

Read the section on heat disease and stop your workout if you sense that you are even beginning to become nauseous, lose concentration or mental awareness of your condition, etc.

- Done on a short running day once a week.
- Do the run-walk ratio that you usually use, going at a very easy pace.
- Warm up with a 5 min walk and take a 5 min walk warm down.
- Temperature should be between 75°F and 85°F (22-27°C) for best results.
- Stop at the first sign of nausea or significant heat stress.
- When less than 70°F (19°C), you can put on additional layers of clothing to simulate a higher temperature.
- First session, run-walk for only 3-4 minutes in the heat.
- Each successive session, add 2-3 minutes.
- Build up to a maximum of 25 minutes—but don't push into heat disease.
- Regularity is important to maintain adaptations—once every week.
- If you miss a week or more, reduce the amount significantly and rebuild.

## Tip: Maintaining heat tolerance during the winter

By putting on additional layers of clothing so that you sweat within 3-4 minutes of your run-walk, you can keep much of your summer heat conditioning that took so much work to produce. Continue to run for a total of 12 minutes or more as you build according to the workout above.

# TROUBLE-SHOOTING

## Times are slowing down at the end

- Your long runs aren't long enough.
- You are running too fast at the beginning of the race.
- You may benefit from walk breaks that are taken more frequently.
- You may be overtrained—back off the speed sessions for a week or two.
- In track workouts, run hardest at the end of the workout.
- Temperature and/or humidity may be to blame—try slowing down at the beginning.

## Slowing down in the middle of the race

- You may be running too hard at the beginning—slow down by a few seconds each lap.
- You may benefit from more frequent walk breaks.
- In track workouts, work the hardest in the middle of the workout.

## Nauseous at the end

- You ran too fast at the beginning.
- Temperature is above 65°F/17°C
- You ate too much before the race or workout—even hours before.
- You ate the wrong foods—most commonly, fat, fried foods, milk products, fibrous foods.

## Tired during workouts

- You are low in B vitamins.
- You are low in iron—have a serum ferritin test.
- You are not eating enough protein.
- Your blood sugar is low before exercise.
- You are not eating within 30 min of the finish of a run.
- You are eating too much fat—especially right after a run.
- You are running too many days per week.
- You are running too hard on long runs.
- You are running too hard on all running days.

# PROBLEMS

## Side Pain

This is very common, and usually has a simple fix. Normally it is not anything to worry about...it just hurts. This condition is due to

1) the lack of deep breathing, and
2) going a little too fast from the beginning of the run.

You can correct #2 easily by walking more at the beginning, and/or slowing down your running pace during the first minute or so.

Deep breathing from the beginning of a run can prevent side pain. This way of inhaling air is performed by diverting the air you breathe into your lower lungs. Also called "belly breathing," this is how we breathe when asleep, and it provides maximum opportunity for oxygen absorption. If you don't deep-breathe when you run, and you are not getting the oxygen you need, the side pain will tell you. By slowing down, walking, and breathing deeply for a while, the pain may go away. But sometimes it does not. Most runners just continue to run and walk with the side pain. In 50 years of running and helping others run, I've not seen any lasting negative effect from those who run with a side pain—it just hurts.

## Tip

Some runners have found that side pain goes away if they tightly grasp a rock in the hand that is on the side of the pain. Squeeze it for 15 seconds or so. Keep squeezing 3-5 times as you breathe deeply.

You don't have to take in a maximum breath to perform this technique. Simply breathe a normal breath, but send it to the lower lungs. You know that you have done this if your stomach goes up and down as you inhale and exhale. If your chest goes up and down, you are breathing shallowly.

## Note

Never breathe in and out rapidly. This can lead to hyperventilation, dizziness, and fainting.

## I feel great one day...and not the next

If you can solve this problem, you could become a very wealthy person. There are a few common reasons for this, but there will always be "those days" when the body doesn't seem to work right, or the gravity seems heavier than normal, and you cannot find a reason. You should keep looking for the causes of this, if you feel this way several times a week, for two or more weeks in a row.

1.  Just do it. In most cases, this is a one-day occurrence. Most runners just put more walking into the mix, slow down, and get through it. Before doing a speed workout, however, make sure that you don't have a medical reason why you feel bad. I've had some of my best workouts after feeling very bad during the first few miles—or the first few speed repetitions.

2.  Heat and/or Humidity will make you feel worse. You will often feel better when the temperature is below 60°F and miserable when 75°F or above—and/or the humidity is low.

3.  Low blood sugar can make any run a bad run. You may feel good at the start, and suddenly feel like you have no energy. Every step seems to take a major effort. Read the chapter in this book about this topic.

4.  Low motivation. Use the rehearsal techniques in the "staying motivated" chapter to get you out the door on a bad day. These have helped numerous runners turn their minds around—even in the middle of a run.

5.  Infection can leave you feeling lethargic, achy, and unable to run at the same pace that was easy a few days

earlier. Check the normal signs (fever, chills, swollen lymph glands, higher morning pulse rate, etc.) and at least call your doctor if you suspect something.

6. Medication and alcohol, even when taken the day before, can leave a hangover that dampens a workout. Your doctor or pharmacist should be able to tell you about the effect of medication on strenuous exercise.

7. A slower start can make the difference between a good day and a bad day. When your body is on the edge of fatigue or other stress, it only takes a few seconds too fast per mile, walking and/or running, to push into discomfort or worse. A quick adjustment to a slightly slower pace before you get too tired can turn this around.

8. Caffeine can help, because it gets the central nervous system working to top capacity. I feel better and my legs work so much better when I have had a cup of coffee an hour before the start of a run. Of course, those who have any problems with caffeine should avoid it—or consult a doctor.

## Cramps in the muscles

At some point, most people who run will experience an isolated cramp. These muscle contractions usually occur in the feet or the calf muscles, and may come during a run or walk, or they may hit at random afterward. Most commonly, they will occur at night, or when you are sitting around at your desk or watching TV in the afternoon or evening. When severe cramps occur during a run, you will have to stop or significantly slow down.

Cramps vary in severity. Most are mild but some can grab so hard that they shut down the muscles and hurt when they seize up. Massage, and a short and gentle movement of the muscle can help to bring most of the cramps around. Odds are that stretching will make the cramp worse, or tear the muscle fibers.

Most cramps are due to overuse—doing more than in the recent past, or continuing to put yourself at your limit, especially in warm weather. Look at the pace and distance of your runs and workouts in your training journal to see if you have been running too far, or too fast, or both.

- Continuous running increases cramping. Taking walk breaks more often can reduce or eliminate cramps. Several runners who used to cramp when they ran continuously stopped cramping with a 10-30 second walk break each lap, or every quarter to half mile of a long or fast run.

- During hot weather, a good electrolyte beverage can help to replace the salts that your body loses in sweating. A drink like Accelerade, for example, can help to top off these minerals by drinking 6-8 oz. every 1-2 hours throughout the day.

- On very long hikes, walks, or runs, however, the continuous sweating, especially when drinking a lot of fluid, can push your sodium levels too low and produce muscle cramping. If this happens regularly, a buffered salt tablet has helped greatly—a product like Succeed.

- Many medications, especially those designed to lower cholesterol, have as one of their known side effects muscle cramps. Runners who use medications and cramp should ask their doctor if there are alternatives.

## Here are several ways of dealing with cramps:

1. Take a longer and more gentle warm-up.
2. Shorten your run segment—or take walk breaks more often.
3. Slow down your walk, and walk more.
4. Shorten your distance on a hot/humid day.
5. Break your run up into two segments.
6. Look at any other exercise that could be causing the cramps.
7. Take a buffered salt tablet at the beginning of your exercise.
8. Don't push off as hard, or bounce as high off the ground.
9. During speed workouts on hot days, walk more during the rest interval.

# Note

If you have high blood pressure or similar problem, ask your doctor before taking any salt product.

## Upset stomach or diarrhea

Sooner or later, virtually every runner has at least one episode with nausea or diarrhea. It comes from the build-up of total stress that you accumulate in your life. Most commonly the triggering event is the stress of running on that day, due to the causes listed below. But stress is the result of many unique conditions within the individual.

Your body produces the nausea/diarrhea (N/D) to get you to reduce the exercise, which will reduce the stress. Here are the common causes.

1. **Running too fast or too far** is the most common cause. Runners are confused about this, because the pace doesn't feel too fast in the beginning. Each person has a level of fatigue that triggers these conditions. Slowing down, and taking more walk breaks will help you manage the problem. Speed training and racing will increase stress very quickly.

2. **Eating too much or too soon before the run.** Your system has to work hard when running, and it is also hard work to digest food. Doing both at the same time raises stress and results in nausea, etc. Having food in your stomach in the process of being digested is an extra stress and a likely target for elimination.

3. **Eating a high fat or high protein diet.** Even one meal that has over 50% of the calories in fat or protein can lead to N/D hours later.

4. **Eating too much the afternoon or evening, the day before.** A big evening meal will still be in the gut the next morning, being digested. When you bounce up and down on a run, which you will, you add stress to the system and can result in N/D.

5. **Heat and humidity** are a major cause of these problems. Some people don't adapt well to even modest heat increases and experience N/D when racing (or doing speed sessions) at the same pace that did not produce the problem in cool weather. In hot conditions,

everyone has a core body temperature increase that will result in significant stress to the system—often causing nausea, and sometimes diarrhea. By slowing down, taking more walk breaks, and pouring water over your head, you can manage this better.

6. **Drinking too much water before a run.** If you have too much water in your stomach, and you are bouncing around, you put stress on the digestive system. Reduce your intake to the bare minimum. Most runners don't need to drink any fluid before a run that is 60 minutes or less.

7. **Drinking too much of a sugar/electrolyte drink.** Water is the easiest substance for the body to process. The addition of sugar and/or electrolyte minerals, as in a sports drink, makes the substance harder to digest. During a run (especially on a hot day) it is best to drink only water.

8. **Drinking too much fluid (especially a sugar drink) too soon after a run.** Even if you are very thirsty, don't gulp down large quantities of any fluid. Try to drink no more than 6-8 oz., every 20 minutes or so. If you are particularly prone to N/D, just take 2-4 sips every 5 minutes or so. When the body is very stressed and tired, it's not a good idea to consume a sugar drink (sports drink, etc.). The extra stress of digesting the sugar can lead to problems.

9. **Don't let running be stressful to you.** Some runners get too obsessed about getting their run in, or running at a specific pace. This adds stress to your life. Relax and let your run diffuse some of the other tensions in your life.

# Headache

There are several reasons why runners get headaches on runs. While uncommon, they happen to the average runner about 1-5 times a year. The extra stress that running puts on the body can trigger a headache on a tough day—even considering the relaxation that comes from the run. Many runners find that a dose of an over-the-counter headache medication takes care of the problem. As always, consult with your doctor about use of medication. Here are the causes/solutions.

*Dehydration*—if you run in the morning, make sure that you hydrate well the day before. Avoid alcohol if you run in the mornings and have headaches. Also watch the salt in your dinner meal the night before. A good sports drink like Accelerade, taken throughout the day the day before, will help to keep your fluid levels and your electrolytes "topped off." If you run in the afternoon, follow the same advice leading up to your run on the day of the run. If you are dehydrated an hour before a run, it doesn't help to drink a huge amount of water at that time—6-8 oz. is fine.

*Medications can often produce dehydration*—there are some medications that make runners more prone to headaches. Check with your doctor.

*Too hot for you*—run at a cooler time of the day (usually in the morning before the sun gets above the horizon). When on a hot run, pour water over your head.

*Being in the sun*—try to stay in the shade as much as possible. Wear a visor not a hat.

*Running a little too fast*—start all runs more slowly; walk more during the first half of the run.

*Running further than you have run in the recent past*—monitor your mileage and don't increase more than about 15% further than you have run on any single run in the recent past.

*Low blood sugar level*—be sure that you boost your BLS with a snack about 30-60 min before you run. If you are used to having it, caffeine in a beverage can sometimes help this situation also.

*If prone to migranes*—generally avoid caffeine, and try your best to avoid dehydration. Talk to your doctor about other possibilities.

*Watch your neck and lower back*—if you have a slight forward lean as you run, you can put pressure on the spine— particularly in the neck and lower back. Read the form chapter in this book and run upright.

# Quick Treatment Tips

## For all injuries:

1. Take 3 days off from running or any activity that could aggravate the area.
2. Avoid any activity that could aggravate the injury.
3. As you return to running, stay below the threshold of further irritation with much more liberal walking.
4. Don't stretch unless you have ilio-tibial band injury. Stretching keeps most injuries from healing.

## Muscle injuries:

1. Call your doctor's office, and see if you can take prescription strength anti-inflammatory medication.
2. See a sports massage therapist who has worked successfully on many runners.

## Tendon and foot injuries

1. Rub a chunk of ice directly on the area for 15 minutes every night (keep rubbing until the area gets numb— about 15 minutes).

## Note

Ice bags, or gel ice don't seem to do any good at all!

2. Foot injuries sometimes are helped by an air cast.

## Knee injuries

1. Call your doctor's office to see if you can take prescription strength anti-inflammatory medication.
2. See if you can do a little gentle walking, sometimes this helps.

3. Sometimes the knee straps can relieve pain; ask your doctor.
4. Get a shoe check to see if you are in the right shoe.
5. If you have internal knee pain, glucosamine supplement may help.

## Shin injuries

1. If the pain gradually goes away as you run on it, there is less worry of a stress fracture. This is probably a shin splint. If you stay below the threshold of irritating the shin muscle, you can run with shin splints as they gradually go away.
2. But if the pain hurts more as you run on it, see a doctor! (possible stress fracture)

## Starting back running before the injury has healed

With most running injuries, you can continue to run even while the injury is healing. But, first you must have some time off to get the healing started. If you do this at the beginning of an injury, you will usually only need 2-5 days off.

The longer you try to push through the problem, the more damage you produce and the longer it will take to heal. Stay in touch with the doctor at any stage of this healing/running process and use your best judgement.

To allow for healing once you have returned to running, stay below the threshold of further irritation. In other words, if the injury feels a little irritated when running at 2.5 miles, and starts hurting a little at 3 miles, you should run no more than 2 miles. And if your run-walk ratio is 3 min run/1 min walk, you should drop back to  1-1 or 30 seconds/30 seconds.

Always allow a day of rest between running days. With most injuries you can cross train to maintain conditioning, but make sure that your injury will allow this. Again, your doctor can advise.

## Best cross training modes to maintain your running conditioning

Before doing any of these ask your doctor. Most are fine for most injuries. But some run a risk of irritating the injured area and delaying the healing process.

For more information on this, see the chapter on cross training in my *Galloway's Book on Running*. Gradually build up the cross training, because you have to condition those muscles gradually also. Even walking is a great way to maintain conditioning, if the injury and the doctor will allow it.

1. Running in the water—can improve your running form
2. Nordic track machines
3. Walking
4. Rowing machines
5. Eliptical machines

There is much more information on specific injuries in my *Galloway's Book on Running*. But here are some helpful items that I want to pass on as one runner to another.

## KNEE PAIN

Most knee problems will go away if you take 5 days off. Ask your doctor if you can use anti-inflammatory medication. Try to figure out what caused the knee problem. Make sure that your running courses don't have a slant or canter. Look at the most worn pair of shoes you have, even walking shoes. If there is wear on the inside of the forefoot, you probably overpronate. If you have repeat issues with knee pain, you may need a foot support or orthotic. If there is pain under the kneecap, or arthritis, the glucosamine/chondroitin products have helped. The best I've found in this category is Joint Maintenance Product by Cooper Complete.

## OUTSIDE OF THE KNEE PAIN—Iliotibial Band Syndrome

This band of fascia acts as a tendon, going down the outside of the leg from the hip to just below the knee. The pain is most commonly felt on the outside of the knee, but can be felt anywhere along the I-T band. I believe this to be a "wobble injury."

When the running muscles get tired, they don't keep you on a straight running track. The I-T band tries to restrain the wobbling motion, but it cannot and gets overused. Most of the feedback I receive from runners and doctors is that once the healing has started (usually a few days off from running), most runners will heal as fast when you run on it as from a complete layoff. It is crucial to stay below the threshold of further irritation.

## Treatment for Ilio-tibial band:

1. Stretching: Stretch before, after, and even during a run.
2. Massage: a good massage therapist can tell whether massage will help and where to massage. The two areas for possible attention are the connecting points of the connective tissue that is tight, and the fascia band itself, in several places.
3. Walking is usually fine, and a tiny bit of running is usually OK.
4. Direct ice massage on the area of pain: 15 minutes of continuous rubbing every night.

## SHIN PAIN—"Shin Splints" or Stress Fracture

Almost always, pain in this area indicates a minor irritation called "shin splints" that allows running and walking as you heal. The greatest pain or irritation during injury is during the start of a run or walk, which gradually lessens or goes away as you run and walk. It takes a while to fully heal, so you must have patience.

Irritation of the inside of the leg coming up from the ankle is called "posterior tibial shin splints," and is often due to over- pronation of the foot (foot rolls in at push-off). When the pain is in the muscle on the front of the lower leg, it is "anterior tibial shin splints." This is very often due to having too long a stride when running, and especially when walking. Downhill terrain should be avoided as much as possible during the healing.

If the pain is in a very specific place, and increases as you run, it could be a more serious problem: a stress fracture. This is unusual for beginning runners, but characteristic of those who do too much, too soon. It can also indicate low bone density. If you even suspect a stress fracture, do not run or do anything stressful on the leg and see a doctor. Stress fractures take weeks of no running and walking, usually wearing a cast. They may also indicate a calcium deficiency.

## HEEL PAIN—Plantar Fascia

*"The most effective treatment is putting your foot in a supportive shoe before your 1st step in the morning."*

This very common injury hurts when you first walk on the foot in the morning. As you get warmed up, it gradually goes away, only to return the next morning. The most important treatment is to put your foot in a supportive shoe, before you step out of bed each morning. Be sure to get a "shoe check" at a technical running store, to make sure that you have the right shoe for your foot. If the pain is felt during the day, and is painful, you should consult with a podiatrist. Usually the doctor will construct a foot support that will surround your arch and heel. This does not always need to be a hard orthotic, and is usually a softer one designed for your foot with build-ups in the right places. The "toe squincher" exercise noted in this book can help provide foot strength that will also support the foot. It takes several weeks for this to take effect. This is another injury that allows for running as you heal, but stay in touch with your doctor.

## BACK OF THE FOOT—Achilles Tendon

The achilles tendon is the narrow band of tendon rising up from the heel and connecting to the calf muscle. It is part of a very efficient mechanical system, acting as a strong rubber band to leverage a lot of work out of the foot, with a little effort from the calf muscle. It is usually injured due to excessive stretching, either through running or through stretching exercises. First, avoid any activity that stretches the tendon in any way. It helps to add a small heel lift to all shoes, which reduces the range of motion. Every night, rub a chunk of ice directly on the tendon. Keep rubbing for about 15 minutes, until the tendon gets numb. Bags of ice or frozen gels don't do any good at all in my opinion. Usually after 3-5 days off from running, the icing takes hold and gets the injury in a healing mode. Anti-inflammatory medication very rarely helps with the Achilles tendon.

## HIP AND GROIN PAIN

There is a variety of elements that could be aggravated in the hip area. Since the hips are not prime movers in running, they are usually abused when you continue to push on, after getting very tired. The hips try to do the work of the leg muscles and are not designed for this.

Ask your doctor about prescription strength anti-inflammatory medication, as this can often speed up recovery. Avoid stretching and any activity that aggravates the area.

## CALF MUSCLE

The calf is the most important muscle for running. It is often irritated by speedwork, and can be pushed into injury by stretching, running too fast when tired, by too many speed sessions without adequate rest between, and sprinting at the end of races or workouts.

Deep tissue massage has been the best treatment for most calf muscle problems. Try to find a very experienced massage therapist who has helped lots of runners with calf problems. This can be painful, but it is about the only way to remove some bio-damage in the muscle.

Don't stretch! Stretching will tear the muscle fibers that are trying to heal. Avoid running hills, and take very frequent walk breaks as you return to running.

## Other books by Jeff Galloway

*Running—Getting Started*, Meyer & Meyer, 2005.
*Galloway's Book on Running*, Shelter Publications, 2nd Ed., 2002.
*New Marathon*, Phidippides Pub., 2000.
*Jeff Galloway's Training Journal*, Phidippides Pub., 1998.

## Photo Credits

**Cover Design:**  Jens Vogelsang

**Cover Photo:**  Stefan Eisend

**Back Cover &
Inside Photos:**  Polar Electro
Brennan Galloway
Westin Galloway
Gregory Sheats
Bakke-Svensson/WTC

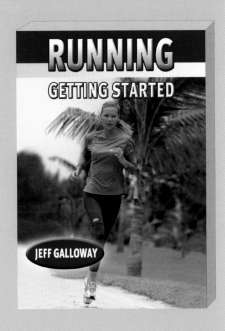

Jeff Galloway
## Running
### Getting Started

"Running—Getting Started" will take anyone, at any level of fitness, into the running lifestyle.

Jeff Galloway, a US Olympian in 1972, has helped over 150,000 people into running while reducing or eliminating aches, pains, and injuries suffered during most training programs.

Jeff offers a step by step program that is easy to use and easy to understand.

Included will be lots of tips on nutrition, staying motivated, building endurance, shoes, stretching and strengthening, and much more.

232 pages, full color print
30 photos and illustrations
Paperback, 5 $^3/4$" x 8 $^1/4$"
ISBN: 1-84126-166-1
c. £ 12.95 UK / $ 17.95 US
$ 26.95 CDN / € 16.95

MEYER & MEYER Sport | sales@m-m-sports.com | www.m-m-sports.com

MEYER & MEYER SPORT

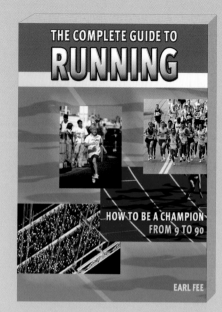

Earl Fee
## The Complete Guide to Running
How to Be a Champion from 9 to 90

This is a book for all fitness enthusiasts from a young age to ninety, those with a dream, those who want to improve, those who want to learn the why and not just the how, and those who dare to excel.

The basic principles of training are applicable to all ages.

With proper training, the body, mind, and spirit are each fully used and all are in harmony. This book aims for this perfection to assist you in the serious play of athletic excellence, and to attain your fullest talents in your sport, especially in running.

440 pages, full color print
50 photos and illustrations
Paperback, 5 $^3$/4" x 8 $^1$/4"
ISBN: 1-84126-162-9
c. £ 17.95 UK / $ 29.00 US
$ 39.95 CDN / € 23.95

MEYER
& MEYER
SPORT

MEYER & MEYER Sport | sales@m-m-sports.com | www.m-m-sports.com

Anz Testing Yourself

Jürg Wirz

## Paul Tergat—
### Running to the Limit
#### His Life and His Training Secrets

This book illustrates Tergat's way from an unknown runner in a tiny village in Kenya to the Marathon world record holder and Dollar-millionaire.

In "Running to the Limit" Paul Tergat also tells a lot about his training program. He gives many training tips for everyday runners, because many of his hints and ideas hold true for record holders as well as for hobbyists.

"Running to the Limit" is richly illustrated with colorful photographs, many of them as yet unpublished shots from Kenya.

224 pages, full color print
400 photos and illustrations
Paperback, 5 $^3/4$" x 8 $^1/4$"
ISBN: 1-84126-165-3
c. £ 12.95 UK / $ 17.95 US
$ 25.95 CDN / € 16.95

MEYER & MEYER Sport | sales@m-m-sports.com | www.m-m-sports.com